SAVING ENDANGERED SPECIES

THE
JAGUAR
Help Save This Endangered Species!

Stephen Feinstein

MyReportLinks.com Books

an imprint of

Enslow Publishers, Inc.

Box 398, 40 Industrial Road
Berkeley Heights, NJ 07922
USA

J
599.755
Feinstein

MyReportLinks.com Books, an imprint of Enslow Publishers, Inc. MyReportLinks® is a registered trademark of Enslow Publishers, Inc.

Library of Congress Cataloging-in-Publication Data

Feinstein, Stephen.
  The jaguar : help save this endangered species! / Stephen Feinstein.
     p. cm. — (Saving endangered species)
  Includes bibliographical references (p.   ) and index.
  ISBN-13: 978-1-59845-065-1
  ISBN-10: 1-59845-065-4
 1. Jaguar—Juvenile literature. I. Title.
QL737.C23F395 2007
599.75'5—dc22

                                  2006027780

Printed in the United States of America

10 9 8 7 6 5 4 3 2

To Our Readers:
Through the purchase of this book, you and your library gain access to the Report Links that specifically back up this book.
The Publisher will provide access to the Report Links that back up this book and will keep these Report Links up to date on **www.myreportlinks.com** for five years from the book's first publication date.
We have done our best to make sure all Internet addresses in this book were active and appropriate when we went to press. However, the author and the Publisher have no control over, and assume no liability for, the material available on those Internet sites or on other Web sites they may link to.
The usage of the MyReportLinks.com Books Web site is subject to the terms and conditions stated on the Usage Policy Statement on **www.myreportlinks.com.**
A password may be required to access the Report Links that back up this book. The password is found on the bottom of page 4 of this book.
Any comments or suggestions can be sent by e-mail to comments@myreportlinks.com or to the address on the back cover.

♻ Enslow Publishers, Inc., is committed to printing our books on recycled paper. The paper in every book contains 10% to 30% post-consumer waste (PCW). The cover board on the outside of each book contains 100% PCW. Our goal is to do our part to help young people and the environment too!

Photo Credits: American Zoo and Aquarium Association, p. 113; Arizona Game & Fish, p. 29; ARKive, p. 66; Audubon, p. 82; Big Cat Rescue, p. 22; Canadian Museum of Civilization, p. 75; © Jeff Carpenter, Shutterstock.com, p. 3; Center for Biological Diversity, p. 105; Clipart.com, p. 97; *Codex Magliabechiano,* p. 92; *Codex Telleriano-Remensis,* pp. 84–85; ©Colman Lerner Gerado, Shutterstock.com, pp. 78–79; © Corel Corporation, pp. 10, 40, 43, 44–45, 50–51, 53, 55, 58–59, 60–61, 83, 90–91, 99; *Defenders,* p. 33; Defenders of Wildlife, p. 13; EFBC/FCC, p. 103; Enslow Publishers, Inc., p. 5; Feline Conservation Center, p. 46; IUCN-World Conservation Union, p. 15; © Jose Adib Cervantes Garcia, Shutterstock, pp. 114–115; Malpai Borderlands Group, p. 112; MyReportLinks.com Books, p. 4; *National Geographic,* pp. 28, 110; National Wildlife Federation, p. 95; The Northern Jaguar Project, p. 31; One World Journeys, p. 81; PBS, pp. 72, 74; Philadelphia Zoo, p. 107; ©Photos.com, p. 38; © Ronnie Howard, Shutterstock.com, pp. 26–27, 68–69; San Diego Zoological Park, p. 62; The Sierra Club, p. 19; © Shutterstock.com, pp. 1, 88; *Smithsonian,* p. 34; Smithsonian National Zoological Park, p. 64; © Joe Stone, Shutterstock.com, pp. 100–101; U.S. Fish and Wildlife Service, pp. 17, 117; Western Alliance for Nature Conservancy, p. 41; Wildlife Conservation Society, pp. 11, 20; World Wildlife Fund, p. 87.

Cover Photograph: © Shutterstock.com

CONTENTS

MyReportLinks.com Books
Great Books, Great Links, Great for Research!

The Internet sites featured in this book can save you hours of research time. These Internet sites—we call them **"Report Links"**—are constantly changing, but we keep them up to date on our Web site.

When you see this "Approved Web Site" logo, you will know that we are directing you to a great Internet site that will help you with your research.

Give it a try! Type http://www.myreportlinks.com into your browser, click on the series title and enter the password, then click on the book title, and scroll down to the Report Links listed for this book.

The Report Links will bring you to great source documents, photographs, and illustrations. MyReportLinks.com Books save you time, feature Report Links that are kept up to date, and make report writing easier than ever! A complete listing of the Report Links can be found on pages 118–119 at the back of the book.

Please see "To Our Readers" on the copyright page for important information about this book, the MyReportLinks.com Web site, and the Report Links that back up this book.

Please enter **JES2567** if asked for a password.

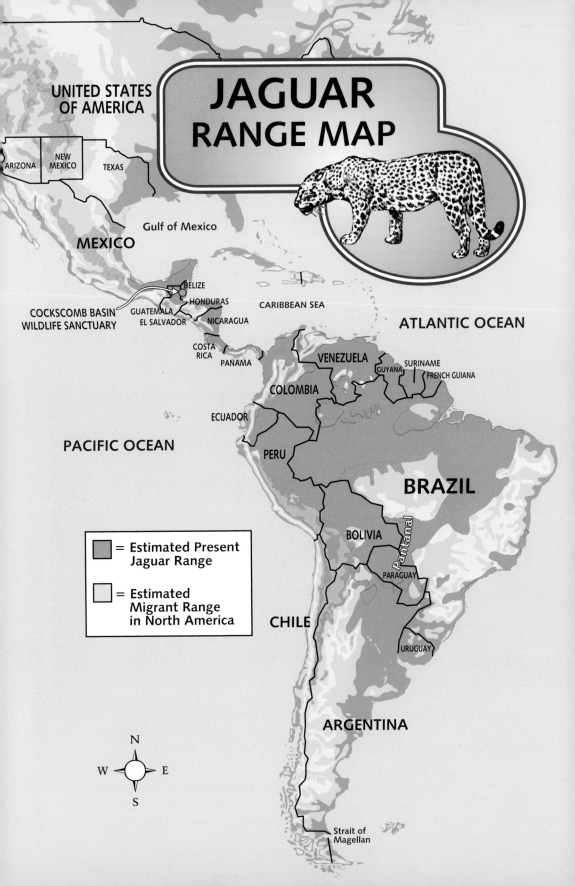

JAGUAR
RANGE MAP

UNITED STATES
OF AMERICA

ARIZONA | NEW MEXICO | TEXAS

Gulf of Mexico

MEXICO

BELIZE

HONDURAS

COCKSCOMB BASIN
WILDLIFE SANCTUARY

GUATEMALA
EL SALVADOR

NICARAGUA

CARIBBEAN SEA

ATLANTIC OCEAN

COSTA
RICA

PANAMA

VENEZUELA

GUYANA

SURINAME

FRENCH GUIANA

COLOMBIA

ECUADOR

PERU

BRAZIL

PACIFIC OCEAN

BOLIVIA

Pantanal

PARAGUAY

= Estimated Present
Jaguar Range

= Estimated
Migrant Range
in North America

CHILE

URUGUAY

ARGENTINA

N
W · E
S

Strait of
Magellan

JAGUAR FACTS

▶ **Scientific Name**
Panthera onca

▶ **Range**
The area spreads from the southwestern United States through Mexico and Central America to Argentina in South America.

▶ **Current Population Estimates**
Much of the jaguar's habitat is inaccessible to humans, so researchers do not have even a rough estimate of the number of jaguars alive today. In 1996, according to statistics compiled by the IUCN Red List, there were thought to be less than fifty thousand jaguars, but that number is probably smaller now due to deforestation and other types of habitat destruction and killings by ranchers.

▶ **Types of Habitats**
Jaguars are found in a great variety of habitats including tropical rain forests, semievergreen forests, dry deciduous forests, swampy grasslands, lowland mangrove swamps, dry areas of scrub and brush, and even desert terrain, as long as there is water in the area.

▶ **Life Span**
A jaguar lives fifteen to twenty years in the wild and up to twenty-five years in captivity.

▶ **Appearance**
Jaguars closely resemble leopards, although the jaguar is sturdier and heavier. Its background coat varies from pale gold to rich golden orange with numerous black rings or rosettes on the back and flanks and spots on the head and neck. Its underbelly is white and is marked with black splotches. The inside of its ears, lower muzzle, jaw, throat, and the inside of its legs are all white or pale gray. Its eyes have round pupils and irises with a golden or reddish-yellow color. Very young cubs have blue eyes. Some jaguars are black, or melanistic (having a dark pigmentation).

▶ **Average Size**
Length: 5.3 to 6 feet (1.62 to 1.83 meters)
Tail: 17.0 to 29.5 inches (43 to 75 centimeters) long
Height at the shoulders: 27 to 30 inches (68.6 to 76 centimeters)
Average Weight: 124 to 211 pounds (56 to 96 kilograms)

▶ **Physical Characteristics**
Jaguars are powerful, ferocious hunters. They have the strongest teeth and jaws of any American cat, including the mountain lion. Jaguars also have razor-sharp front claws. Unlike other big cats that kill their prey by

biting the neck, jaguars bite the skull, piercing the brain. Jaguars are solitary hunters.

▶ Home Range

A jaguar's home range can vary from 15 to 90 square miles (39 to 233 square kilometers). The size depends on the habitat, availability of prey, and the animal's sex, because male home ranges are about twice as large as those of females. Male and female ranges do overlap. Jaguars are territorial, marking their territory by placing scent marks on bushes or scratches on trees.

▶ Sensory Systems

Jaguars have extremely sensitive eyes and ears. Their pupils dilate widely to gather as much light as possible in the dark. There is a special layer of reflecting cells at the back of the eyes called the tapetum, which acts like a mirror. Some of the light rays that reach the jaguar's eyes pass through the retina without being absorbed by the light-sensitive receptor cells. This light bounces off the tapetum and is then absorbed by the retina, doubling the sensitivity of the jaguar's eyes.

▶ Locomotion

Jaguars have short, muscular legs and strong shoulders that have adapted to give the animal the strength and agility to crawl, swim, and climb.

▶ Communication

The jaguar is the only cat in the Americas that can roar. The roar could be a mating call or a kind of territorial marking. Jaguars growl and mew on occasion and will snarl when cornered by dogs.

▶ Reproduction

Female jaguars become sexually mature between two and three years of age and males between three and four years. Jaguars can mate at any time of year, but mating is usually timed so that births will occur during the rainy season, when prey is more abundant. The gestation period, the time when the female carries her unborn, is about three months. A litter averages two cubs, but can be up to four.

▶ Diet

Jaguars are carnivorous, meaning they are meat eaters. Their diet consists of more than eighty species of animals, including capybaras, tapirs, peccaries, armadillos, caimans, iguanas, turtles, fish, deer, otters, lizards, frogs, small rodents, birds, sloths, monkeys, and snakes.

▶ Threats

They include illegal hunting, loss of habitat due to human settlement, agricultural development, mining, logging, cattle ranching, and road building.

We sit by and allow massive destruction of the jaguar's habitat, forcing it into situations where death is the inevitable conclusion. Yet even as we are destroying it, we admire the animal . . . and we wonder how it lives. . . .

—Dr. Alan Rabinowitz

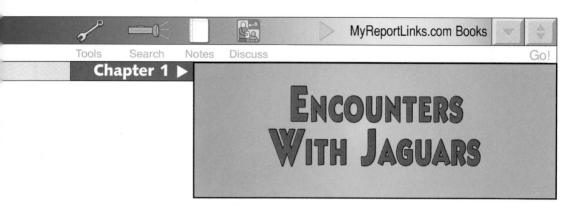

ENCOUNTERS WITH JAGUARS

The jaguar *(Panthera onca)* is the largest and most powerful cat in the Americas and the third largest cat in the world. Closely related to the tigers, lions, and leopards of Asia and Africa, the jaguar is found only in North, Central, and South America, mainly in warm regions. It ranges from the southwestern United States south to Argentina in South America. Although, sadly, there are no longer any breeding populations of jaguars in the United States.

For thousands of years, some ancient cultures of Mexico and Central and South America regarded the jaguar as a symbol of power and strength. They believed that the jaguar had a special connection to the spirit world. These ancient peoples admired, honored, and even worshipped this big cat. To the Maya, the jaguar's spotted skin symbolized the stars in the night sky. The Aztec sacrificed human victims and fed their hearts to jaguars.

Today in Mexico, people still look upon the jaguar with awe. According to the naturalist and writer Aldo Starker Leopold, who researched and wrote about the wildlife of Mexico, "The chesty

To many of the ancient cultures of Mexico and Central America, the jaguar represented power and strength. Despite that strength, however, the biggest cat of the Americas is endangered.

roar of a jaguar in the night causes men to edge toward the blaze and draw serapes tighter. It silences the yapping dogs and starts the tethered horses milling. In announcing its mere presence in the blackness of night, the jaguar puts the animate world on edge."[1]

Back in 1883, the scientist Charles Darwin visited South America on his famous voyage aboard the *Beagle*. One of his trips on shore was cut short when it became apparent that a jaguar might be lurking nearby. Darwin confessed that "the fear of the [jaguar] quite destroyed all pleasure in scrambling through the woods. I had not proceeded a hundred yards before finding

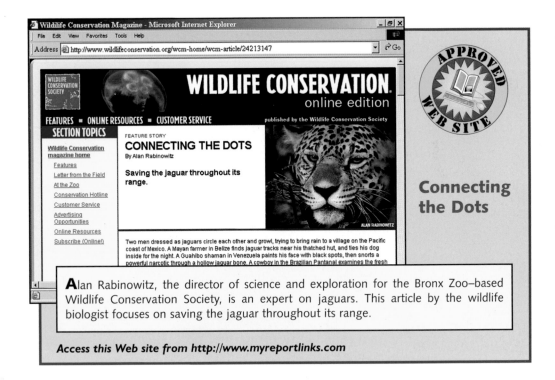

Alan Rabinowitz, the director of science and exploration for the Bronx Zoo–based Wildlife Conservation Society, is an expert on jaguars. This article by the wildlife biologist focuses on saving the jaguar throughout its range.

Access this Web site from http://www.myreportlinks.com

indubitable signs. . . . I was obliged to come back."[2]

Dr. Alan Rabinowitz, now the director of science and exploration for the Wildlife Conservation Society, has long been a great admirer of the jaguar. He spent years studying the big cats in their natural habitat in the jungles of Belize. There he helped establish the world's first jaguar preserve, which opened in 1984. Dr. Rabinowitz wrote vivid descriptions of his encounters with jaguars. In one incident, he released a captive jaguar from its cage on a truck. Rabinowitz had expected the big cat to run away into the jungle. But, instead, the jaguar stopped and turned toward him. Their eyes met, and Rabinowitz knew he was in danger. Suddenly the jaguar came at Rabinowitz, who leaped up into the rear of the truck. The jaguar jumped too. Rabinowitz "screamed, feeling for an instant what the weaker animal must feel before it's killed."[3]

Fortunately, the jaguar's jump fell short of the truck. Rabinowitz described what happened next:

> I waited for the next jump, which would easily bring him within striking distance. The crushed skulls of jaguar prey flashed through my mind. But the next leap never occurred. He stood up, looked at me, then turned and walked slowly into the forest.
>
> I watched as he disappeared from sight, staring at the spot where the forest had absorbed him. I was shaking uncontrollably and my head was

Jaguar - Defenders of Wildlife - Windows Internet Explorer

http://www.defenders.org/programs_and_policy/wildlife_conservation/imperil

File Edit View Favorites Tools Help

Jaguar - Defenders of Wildlife

Donate : Renew : Free eNews Sign Up | Text size: A A A | Search Our Site

Defenders of Wildlife

Home | About Us | Newsroom | Support Us | Programs & Policy | Wildlife & Habitat | Take Action | Resources

Home > Programs and Policy > Wildlife Conservation > Imperiled Species
> Jaguar
Email Print +Share

Programs and Policy

Imperiled Species

Jaguar

Background and
Recovery

In the Field

Management and
Policy

Publications and
Facts

Defenders' Experts

Jaguar

The jaguar (Panthera onca) is the largest cat native to North America and the third largest cat in the world. In the U.S.-Mexico borderlands the unique American jaguar has been virtually eliminated from its entire U.S. range, but Defenders and its partners are working hard to save remaining populations in Mexico.

Read Background and Recovery

Sea Otter

Defenders in Your World

Choose an animal or habitat

Choose a state or region

DEFENDING WOLVE

Defenders of
Wildlife led
the effort to
reintroduce
wolves to
Yellowstone
National

Jaguar

This conservation organization's site provides information on jaguars and discusses its three-point strategy to bring the big cats back to the American Southwest.

Access this Web site from http://www.myreportlinks.com

pounding. What an animal, I thought. Even in the aftermath of abject terror, I couldn't help but feel admiration for that jaguar. I named him Kukulcán, after the king who ruled over the last great centers of the Maya Indians before their final collapse.[4]

▶ The Jaguar: An Endangered Species

Scientists today believe we are witnessing a mass extinction of many of the world's species of animals and plants. This ongoing, destructive process is unfortunately due to the presence and activities of human beings. Wild species in many areas are facing the shrinkage and sometimes complete loss of their natural habitats. Humans have moved into these formerly wild areas, settling and exploiting the land for a variety of uses. The establishment of farms, the building of roads, and the activities of ranching, logging, and mining have drastically changed the environment where jaguars live.

Even though jaguars range across large geographical areas, they have suffered significant loss of habitat. This has mainly occurred in the United States, Mexico, Brazil, and Argentina. Jaguars have traditionally been hunted whenever they came close to areas where humans lived. Ranchers saw the big cats as threats to themselves, their livestock, and their pets. Hunters killed not only the jaguars, but also many of the animals that jaguars prey upon. The lack of prey meant that the jaguar population also suffered. Huge numbers of jaguars were also killed by hunters working in the fur trade, to sell the cats' pelts.

▶ What "Endangered" Means

Sadly, like so many other species of animals, the awesome jaguar became an endangered species. In 1973, the Endangered Species Act (ESA) was voted into law by the U.S. Congress. The purpose of the law is "to provide a means whereby the ecosystems upon which endangered species and threatened species depend may be conserved, to provide a program for the conservation of such endangered species and threatened species."[5] That year the

IUCN Red List of Threatened Species: Panthera onca - Microsoft Internet Explorer

File   Edit   View   Favorites   Tools   Help

Address   http://www.iucnredlist.org/search/details.php/15953/all   Go

The IUCN Red List of
Threatened Species™

**Species
Information**

Was this information useful? Support the Red List here.

Panthera onca

Summary | Distribution | Other Documentation | References | **Comprehensive**

Taxonomy	
Kingdom	ANIMALIA
Phylum	CHORDATA
Class	MAMMALIA
Order	CARNIVORA
Family	FELIDAE
Common Name/s	JAGUAR (E, F, S) OTORONGO (S)

On the Web site of the **IUCN Red List of Threatened Species,** a searchable database listing the world's endangered animals and plants, browsers can find information on the jaguar, *Panthera onca.*

United States government officially began making a list of endangered and threatened species, and the jaguar was listed as an endangered species.

▷ The ESA and IUCN

The Endangered Species Act defines an endangered species as one that is in immediate danger of becoming extinct throughout most of its range. The jaguar is currently listed as endangered in its entire range. That range includes Arizona, New Mexico, Texas, Mexico, and Central and South

America. Threatened species are defined as those that could become endangered in the near future. The first list in 1973 included seventy-seven species. Today, 1,256 animal and plant species are being considered as candidates for the list. In addition, thousands more are considered by states, environmental groups, and scientists as "species of concern" or "critically imperiled."

Meanwhile, the IUCN-World Conservation Union has been maintaining its own list of endangered species. In May 2006, the IUCN released an update of their Red List of Threatened Species—in this case, "threatened" includes animals in danger of extinction. More than 40 percent (16,119 species) of the 40,177 species assessed by the IUCN are threatened with extinction. These include one in four mammals, one in eight birds, one in three amphibians, and a quarter of the world's coniferous (cone-bearing) trees.

▶ CITES

On March 3, 1973, representatives of eighty nations gathered in Washington, D.C., at a meeting of the IUCN. They agreed on the text of CITES, the Convention on International Trade in Endangered Species of Wild Fauna and Flora. CITES is an international agreement between participating governments to ensure that any trade (selling or buying) of wild animals and plants

ENDANGERED SPECIES PROGRAM KID'S CORNER - Microsoft Internet Explorer

File Edit View Favorites Tools Help

Address http://www.fws.gov/endangered/kids/index.html   Go

U.S. Fish & Wildlife Service

Kid's Corner

Endangered Means There Is Still Time
Species Spotlight | How Can Kids Help? | Educators
Learn More | Endangered Species Program

Endangered Means There is Still Time

USFWS Endangered Species Program Kid's Corner

On this page, the United States Fish and Wildlife Service (USFWS), which is responsible for protecting endangered species, offers ways in which you can become involved in saving those species and our environment.

Access this Web site from http://www.myreportlinks.com

does not threaten their survival—in other words, the trade of animals or plants at risk of extinction. In 1973, jaguars were listed in Appendix I of CITES, making it illegal to trade their skins or any of their parts for commercial gain. (Species listed in Appendix II of CITES can be traded commercially only if trade does not harm their survival.)

CITES went into force on July 1, 1975. Today, CITES has 171 members. Each nation that signed the agreement is responsible for enacting laws that make sure that CITES is put into practice at the national level. Thanks to the jaguar's inclusion on the Endangered Species List and CITES, it is now illegal to hunt the big cats. Unfortunately, illegal killing of jaguars continues in many areas.

How You Can Help Save This Species

One of the most useful ways to save jaguars and all endangered species is to learn as much about them as you can and share that knowledge with friends and family. It is only through knowledge that you and others can learn how important all creatures are to our planet's welfare. Once people begin to care about jaguars and other species at risk of extinction, they can act to help save these endangered species.

You could begin by asking your representatives in Congress to support the Great Cats and Rare Canids Act of 2007. This act will provide much-needed funding to international conservation efforts aimed at ensuring the survival of thirteen species of great cats and rare canines. These thirteen endangered or threatened species are the lion, tiger, leopard, jaguar, snow leopard, clouded leopard, cheetah, Iberian lynx, dhole, gray wolf, Ethiopian wolf, African wild dog, and maned wolf. Individually or as a class project, contact your congressional representatives and ask them to support the Great Cats and Rare Canids Act.

You can also urge Congress to support funding of the Biodiversity Program at the U.S. Agency for International Development (USAID) and the Global Environment Facility (GEF). These are the primary

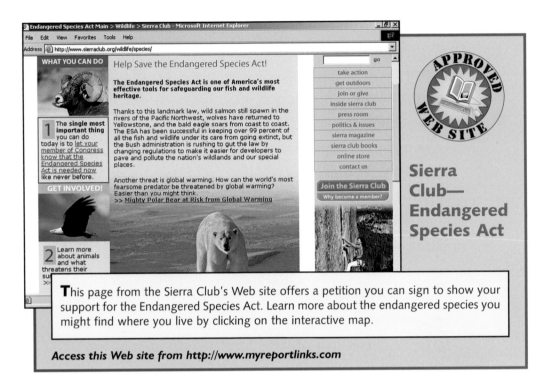

Endangered Species Act Main > Wildlife > Sierra Club - Microsoft Internet Explorer

File   Edit   View   Favorites   Tools   Help

Address http://www.sierraclub.org/wildlife/species/

WHAT YOU CAN DO

1 The **single most important thing** you can do today is to let your member of Congress know that the Endangered Species Act is needed now like never before.

GET INVOLVED!

2 Learn more about animals and what threatens their sur...

Help Save the Endangered Species Act!

The Endangered Species Act is one of America's most effective tools for safeguarding our fish and wildlife heritage.

Thanks to this landmark law, wild salmon still spawn in the rivers of the Pacific Northwest, wolves have returned to Yellowstone, and the bald eagle soars from coast to coast. The ESA has been successful in keeping over 99 percent of all the fish and wildlife under its care from going extinct, but the Bush administration is rushing to gut the law by changing regulations to make it easier for developers to pave and pollute the nation's wildlands and our special places.

Another threat is global warming. How can the world's most fearsome predator be threatened by global warming? Easier than you might think.
>> Mighty Polar Bear at Risk from Global Warming

go

take action
get outdoors
join or give
inside sierra club
press room
politics & issues
sierra magazine
sierra club books
online store
contact us

Join the Sierra Club
Why become a member?

APPROVED WEB SITE

Sierra
Club—
Endangered
Species Act

This page from the Sierra Club's Web site offers a petition you can sign to show your support for the Endangered Species Act. Learn more about the endangered species you might find where you live by clicking on the interactive map.

Access this Web site from http://www.myreportlinks.com

sources of funding for international environmental conservation. The USAID Biodiversity Program and the GEF support environmental programs around the world, especially in developing nations. The biodiversity projects include efforts to save wildlife and habitats (biodiversity conservation), marine conservation, and management of natural resources. There are also projects involving the development of renewable energy sources and energy efficiency.

Save the Endangered Species Act (ESA)

Another important thing you can do to protect not only the jaguar but also other endangered species is to support the Endangered Species Act by letting your representatives and senators know that you consider it important. As the most far-reaching environmental legislation ever passed, the ESA has helped to save the bald eagle, the peregrine falcon, the gray wolf, and other species from disappearing from the earth forever. Recently, some members of Congress have tried to pass legislation that will weaken the act because it would do away with the ESA's mandate of critical habitat. If we do not save the places where these animals live, the animals will die out.

Another way to help the jaguar is to write a letter to the editor of your local newspaper. In the

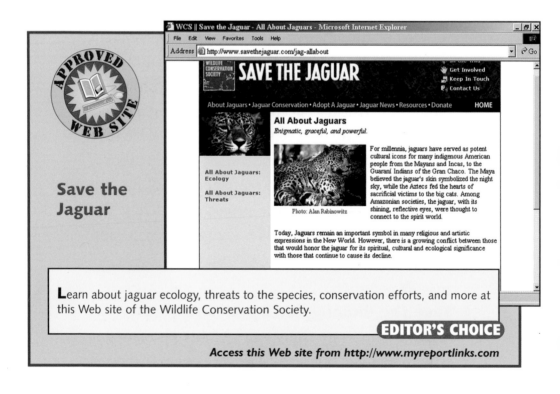

Learn about jaguar ecology, threats to the species, conservation efforts, and more at this Web site of the Wildlife Conservation Society.

Save the Jaguar

EDITOR'S CHOICE

Access this Web site from http://www.myreportlinks.com

letter, point out that the Endangered Species Act works very effectively to protect endangered species, and that Congress should work to strengthen, rather than weaken the law. The Endangered Species Act has prevented 99 percent of all the wildlife, fish, and plants placed under its care from going extinct. It has helped secure a future for hundreds of native plants and animals.

You can also write editorials in support of conservation, especially in matters relating to jaguars. Submit your editorials to your school newspaper and to your local newspapers. Another way to help protect the jaguar is to set up an information table at your school to tell people about the threat of extinction facing jaguars. You can get useful information about jaguars from the Wildlife Conservation Society (WCS) at the Bronx Zoo in New York City. The WCS Web site is one of the links this book recommends. Find it at **www.myreportlinks.com**.

▶ Support Conservation Groups

Nonprofit conservation organizations are working to save the jaguar and other big cats from extinction. These organizations have ongoing fund-raising activities and welcome donations. You can contribute any amount of money—a $5 donation is just as welcome as a $5,000 donation. Encourage your parents and friends to make charitable contributions to any of these organizations, and consider

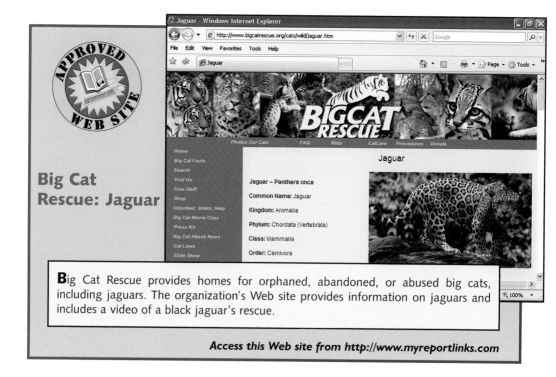

Big Cat Rescue: Jaguar

Jaguar - Windows Internet Explorer

http://www.bigcatrescue.org/cats/wild/jaguar.htm

File   Edit   View   Favorites   Tools   Help

Jaguar

BIGCAT RESCUE

Photos Our Cats   FAQ   Kids   CatCare   Procedures   Donate

Jaguar

Home
Big Cat Facts
Search
Visit Us   **Jaguar – Panthera onca**
Free Stuff
Shop   **Common Name:** Jaguar
Volunteer, Intern, Help
Big Cat Movie Clips   **Kingdom:** Animalia
Press Kit   **Phylum:** Chordata (Vertebrata)
Big Cat Attack News
Cat Laws   **Class:** Mammalia
Slide Show   **Order:** Carnivora

Big Cat Rescue provides homes for orphaned, abandoned, or abused big cats, including jaguars. The organization's Web site provides information on jaguars and includes a video of a black jaguar's rescue.

Access this Web site from http://www.myreportlinks.com

organizing a class fund-raising project at your school with your teacher's permission.

The Wildlife Conservation Society (WCS) has established the Jaguar Conservation Program not only to save jaguars but also to ensure the long-term survival of distinct populations of jaguars scattered across vast stretches of the Americas. The WCS has contributed to jaguar-related research in Argentina, Brazil, Peru, Bolivia, Venezuela, Colombia, Panama, Costa Rica, Honduras, Nicaragua, Belize, Guatemala, Mexico, and the United States. The WCS also has an "adopt-a-jaguar" program. In this program, a monetary donation entitles you to information about the animals you have helped save.

Big Cat Rescue in Tampa, Florida, is another conservation organization working to save jaguars. It has established a sanctuary for jaguars and other big cats that have been abandoned, orphaned, or abused. There are now more than one hundred fifty big cats at the sanctuary. Big Cat Rescue, like WCS, has an adopt-a-jaguar program. Your "adoption" donation is really a sponsorship. The money goes for the care and protection of the jaguar. Your contribution can definitely make a difference in a jaguar's quality of life.

JAGUAR HABITAT AND RANGE, PAST AND PRESENT

Scientists believe that the jaguar *(Panthera onca),* which today can only be found in the Americas, originated somewhere in Eurasia. The *Panthera* ancestor of today's jaguar first began migrating to North America nearly 2 million years ago. Other animals that migrated to North America around this time were mammoths, shrub oxen, and bighorn sheep.

Scientists refer to that geological time period as the Pleistocene Era. There was a series of four ice ages during that period of the earth's history. During each ice age, there were several advances and retreats of the vast ice sheets that formed in northern latitudes. Some scientists believe the ice ages were caused by a slight change in the angle in which the earth was tilted toward the sun. Others believe there might have been variations in the sun's energy output. Whatever the reason, the colder climate caused sea levels to drop 300 to 400 feet (91 to 122 meters). A land bridge called Beringia emerged from the Bering Strait, which separates Asia from North America. Wild animals migrated across this 50-mile-long (80-kilometer-long) land bridge connecting eastern Siberia and Alaska.

Much later, possibly beginning about thirty-five thousand years ago during the most recent ice age, humans migrated across the land bridge from Asia. They were nomadic hunters following the herds of wild animals.

Evolution of the Jaguar

About six hundred thousand years ago, *Panthera onca augusta,* a larger version of today's jaguar, was roaming throughout much of North America and had begun to wander through Central and South America. By this time, the jaguar had separated from other species of *Panthera,* such as the lion *(Panthera leo)* and the tiger *(Panthera tigris).*

Scientists have discovered the fossil remains of *Panthera onca augusta* in California, Washington, Alaska, Pennsylvania, Texas, New Mexico, and Arizona, and in Sonora, Mexico. Sharing the prehistoric jaguar's habitat were animals such as mammoths, tapirs, prehistoric peccaries, extinct pronghorns, and giant ground sloths.[1] Scientists have recovered the fossil remains of seventy-six of the large prehistoric jaguars at the La Brea Tar Pits in Los Angeles. The La Brea Tar Pits also contain fossils of lions and saber-toothed tigers and many other animals.

The La Brea Tar Pits are the richest deposit of ice-age fossils in the world. The tar pits formed when oil from deep underground oozed to the

Scientists believe that the ancestors of the modern jaguar first came to the Americas about 2 million years ago.

🔺 Jaguars @ nationalgeographic.com - Microsoft Internet Explorer   _ ⑤ ✕

File   Edit   View   Favorites   Tools   Help

Address 🔺 http://www.nationalgeographic.com/ngm/0105/feature2/zoom1.html   ▼ ⌀ Go

ZOOM IN

More photos from

Jaguars

<< Back to Feature Page

View exclusive photographs
and get the facts behind the
frame.

Click to ZOOM IN >>

Click to ZOOM IN >>

Catcall
Photograph by Steve Winter

A wildlife warden in Brazil's Pantanal region "roars" into a bucket to call a jaguar. This image and others are featured on the **Phantoms of the Night** Web site, a companion to a *National Geographic* film about the elusive big cat of the Americas.

EDITOR'S CHOICE

surface. Mixing with oxygen, the oil thickened and formed a sticky black tar. When it rained, the water collected on top of the tar, forming a series of ponds or water holes. The large jaguars and the other wild animals in the area did not realize that each water hole was a trap—a tar pit. When the animals went into the water to bathe and drink, their feet got stuck in the tar. They became trapped and stayed there until they died. Eventually, the animal bones became fossilized in the tar pits.

Panthera onca augusta thrived in ancient forests. When the forests in what is now southern California gave way to grasslands and savannas later, the jaguar retreated southward and eastward.

Between fifteen thousand and ten thousand years ago, jaguars in North America diminished in size. Scientists believe this may have resulted from the increasing dryness of the environment as well as the decreasing size of the jaguar's prey. The size and power of predators are related to the size and power of the prey they live on. So when the prey became smaller, the jaguar needed to be strong and fast enough to catch it. Somehow the jaguar managed to survive in the Americas, while other

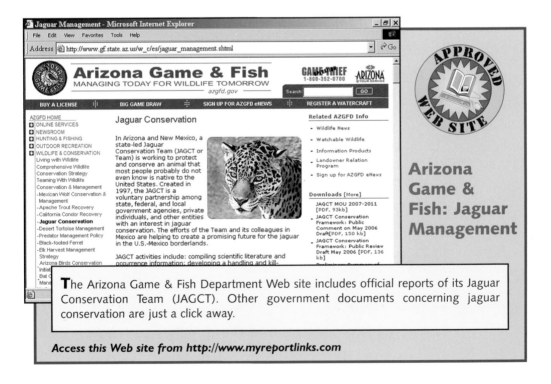

Arizona Game & Fish: Jaguar Management

The Arizona Game & Fish Department Web site includes official reports of its Jaguar Conservation Team (JAGCT). Other government documents concerning jaguar conservation are just a click away.

Access this Web site from http://www.myreportlinks.com

big cats did not. The lion *(Panthera leo)* became extinct in the Americas between ten thousand and eleven thousand years ago.

Where Jaguars Live

The naturalist Aldo Leopold, who observed jaguars in Mexico in the 1950s, wrote:

> The big cat is most at home in the tall shady forests along streams and watercourses that transverse the coastal lowlands. . . . They are particularly prone to follow the big rivers on their northern peregrinations [journeys]—the Brazos, Pecos, Rio Grande, Gila, and Colorado.[2]

In Central America, jaguars can still be found in remote areas of Panama, Costa Rica, eastern Nicaragua, northern and eastern Honduras, northern Guatemala, and Belize. That country is also home to the Cockscomb Basin Wildlife Sanctuary and Jaguar Preserve, the only jaguar sanctuary in the world, established by Dr. Alan Rabinowitz in 1984.

Sizable populations of jaguars can be found in parts of South America, especially in Venezuela, Brazil, Ecuador, and the Guianas. A number of national parks and preserves have been established in these areas, and jaguars find protection in them.

Jaguar Habitat

In the areas of Central and South America where jaguars live, they can be found in many types of

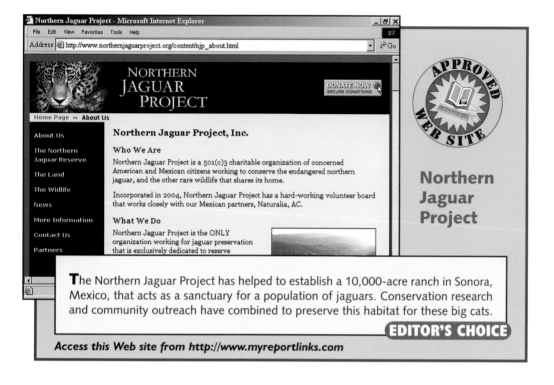

The Northern Jaguar Project has helped to establish a 10,000-acre ranch in Sonora, Mexico, that acts as a sanctuary for a population of jaguars. Conservation research and community outreach have combined to preserve this habitat for these big cats.

EDITOR'S CHOICE

Access this Web site from http://www.myreportlinks.com

tropical forest habitat. These include evergreen rain forests, semievergreen forest, and dry deciduous forest. Jaguars can mostly be found lurking near lowland lakes and rivers where prey is abundant. Because jaguars tend to avoid open country, they become rare as the forests thin out with increasing elevation. Jaguars do not inhabit the Andes and other mountain ranges above 8,500 feet (2,590 meters).

Although jaguars tend to prefer tropical forest habitats, they also live in marshy and even desert terrain. Jaguars thrive in the swampy grasslands of an area of Brazil known as the Pantanal, living around the marshy borders of river systems.

Fragmented populations of the big cats live in Mexico's lowland mangrove forests and swamps. They also dwell in that country's semievergreen forested uplands. There the jaguars hunt prey in forests of oaks, junipers, and pines.

Some of the jaguars that inhabit the borderland of northern Mexico and the few that roam the American Southwest are montane animals. The montane habitat consists of relatively cool, moist upland slopes covered by evergreen forests. A jaguar was killed by a hunter at an elevation of 9,500 feet (2,895 meters) in Arizona's White Mountains. Most borderland jaguars, however, live at lower elevations, ranging from 1,500 to 3,100 feet (457 to 945 meters). This dry country is covered with a type of vegetation known as Sinaloan thornscrub. Jaguars that inhabit areas of scrub and arid brush seldom roam far from water. They have also been observed in semidesert grassland in southern Arizona.

▶ Where Jaguars Are No Longer Found

In many places where they once lived, though, jaguars have been hunted to extinction or near extinction. In South America, jaguars were eliminated from Uruguay by 1900. In Argentina, the last of the jaguars inhabiting the pampas, an area of treeless grassy plains, was killed by 1925. According to research gathered by the Wildlife

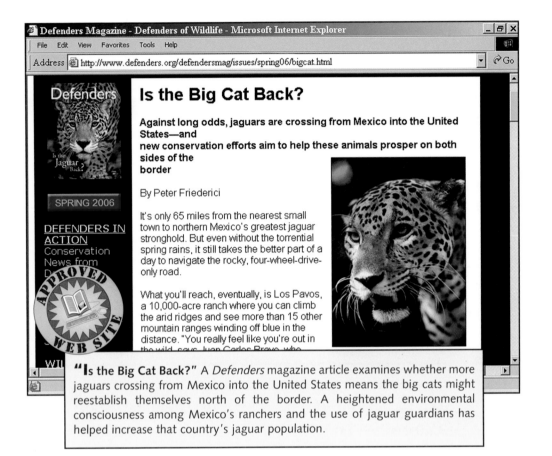

Defenders Magazine - Defenders of Wildlife - Microsoft Internet Explorer

File Edit View Favorites Tools Help

Address http://www.defenders.org/defendersmag/issues/spring06/bigcat.html Go

Defenders

Is the
Jaguar
Back?

SPRING 2006

DEFENDERS IN
ACTION
Conservation
News from

WII

Is the Big Cat Back?

**Against long odds, jaguars are crossing from Mexico into the United States—and
new conservation efforts aim to help these animals prosper on both sides of the
border**

By Peter Friederici

It's only 65 miles from the nearest small town to northern Mexico's greatest jaguar stronghold. But even without the torrential spring rains, it still takes the better part of a day to navigate the rocky, four-wheel-drive-only road.

What you'll reach, eventually, is Los Pavos, a 10,000-acre ranch where you can climb the arid ridges and see more than 15 other mountain ranges winding off blue in the distance. "You really feel like you're out in the wild, says Juan Carlos Bravo, who

"Is the Big Cat Back?" A *Defenders* magazine article examines whether more jaguars crossing from Mexico into the United States means the big cats might reestablish themselves north of the border. A heightened environmental consciousness among Mexico's ranchers and the use of jaguar guardians has helped increase that country's jaguar population.

Conservation Society, jaguars have been lost from over 50 percent of their historical range since 1900. Most of this loss has occurred in Mexico and the United States in the north, and in Brazil and Argentina in the south.

▷ Holding Out in Mexico

Although some of the jaguar's habitat in Mexico and in Central America has been developed and destroyed, jaguars remain in various locations. In southern Mexico, sizable populations of jaguars

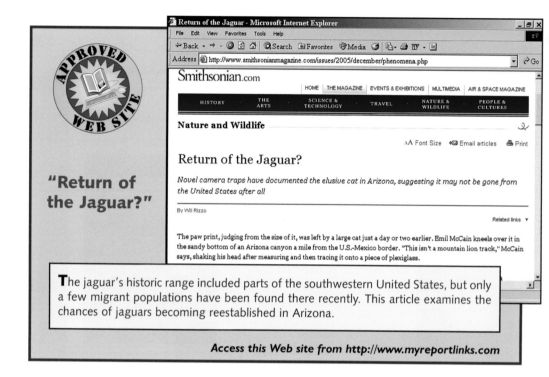

Smithsonian.com

HOME | THE MAGAZINE | EVENTS & EXHIBITIONS | MULTIMEDIA | AIR & SPACE MAGAZINE

HISTORY   ·   THE ARTS   ·   SCIENCE & TECHNOLOGY   ·   TRAVEL   ·   NATURE & WILDLIFE   ·   PEOPLE & CULTURES

Nature and Wildlife

AA Font Size   ◖⊠ Email articles   🖶 Print

Return of the Jaguar?

Novel camera traps have documented the elusive cat in Arizona, suggesting it may not be gone from the United States after all

By Will Rizzo

Related links ▾

The paw print, judging from the size of it, was left by a large cat just a day or two earlier. Emil McCain kneels over it in the sandy bottom of an Arizona canyon a mile from the U.S.-Mexico border. "This isn't a mountain lion track," McCain says, shaking his head after measuring and then tracing it onto a piece of plexiglass.

"Return of the Jaguar?"

The jaguar's historic range included parts of the southwestern United States, but only a few migrant populations have been found there recently. This article examines the chances of jaguars becoming reestablished in Arizona.

Access this Web site from http://www.myreportlinks.com

can be found in the states of Quintana Roo, Campeche, and Chiapas. Jaguars also inhabit remote areas of the states of Oaxaca, Michoacán, Guerrero, Jalisco, Nayarit, and Sinaloa and can be found in other parts of Mexico.

▷ Transients in the United States

Jaguars can occasionally still be found in parts of the American Southwest, but breeding populations no longer live in the United States. Historically, jaguars were found in Arizona, California, Louisiana, New Mexico, and Texas. In 1855, James Capen "Grizzly" Adams, a trapper, came across two jaguars and a cub in the

Tehachapi Mountains of southern California. Adams became famous for traveling around the wilderness in the company of a tame grizzly bear. Adams described one of the jaguars he saw: "The male beast, as nearly as I could see, was twice as large as the ordinary cougar, and appeared to be covered with dark round spots of great richness and beauty. His mien [appearance] was erect and stately, and so majestic and proud in bearing, that it was with pleasure I contemplated him."[3] But jaguars no longer roam California and Louisiana. The last California jaguar was killed in Palm Springs in 1860.

The Decline of *el Tigre* in the United States

In the 1800s, jaguars were reported to be common in southern Texas. Sam Houston, who helped Texas gain its independence from Mexico and was its first president when it was a republic, spoke of seeing jaguars on the headwaters of some of the Rio Grande's tributaries. Scientists believe that the few jaguars seen today in the southwestern United States are lone wanderers from breeding populations of jaguars south of the border.

However, it is possible that in the past, breeding populations of jaguars did inhabit Arizona and perhaps other areas. While there are no "jaguar" place-names in Arizona or New Mexico, several places in Arizona have the word *leopard, tiger,* or *tigre.* This would seem to indicate the presence of jaguars at some time in the past, because Spanish explorers in the Americas referred to the jaguar as *el tigre,* "the tiger." Throughout Mexico and the other Spanish-speaking countries of Latin America, the jaguar is still known as *el tigre.* Its English name "jaguar" is believed to come from the word *yaguara* in the Tupi-Guarani language of the Amazon region of Brazil. *Yaguara* has been translated to mean "eater of us," "body of a dog," and more recently "the wild beast that overcomes its prey at a bound."[4] Unfortunately, it is that image of the jaguar as ferocious that has made so many fear it—and kill it.

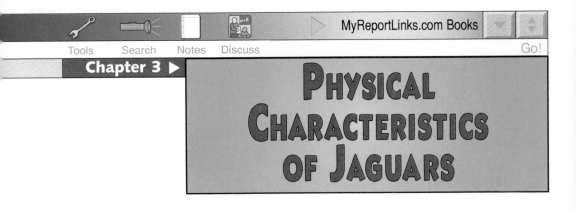

Chapter 3 ▶

PHYSICAL CHARACTERISTICS OF JAGUARS

The jaguar *(Panthera onca)*, the largest big cat in the Americas, looks very much like the leopard *(Panthera pardus)*. Until about 1920, settlers in the American Southwest often referred to the jaguar as an "American leopard" or "Mexican leopard." But leopards are native to Africa and Asia, not the Americas.

Although there is a close resemblance between the two species, jaguars are sturdier and heavier than leopards. The background of their coat can vary from pale gold to a rich golden orange. Jaguars that do not live in forested areas tend to have a slightly lighter orange coat than those that live in the forests. There are numerous black rings or rosettes on the back and flanks, while the head and neck are spotted. Along the middle of the jaguar's back, a row of black spots may merge into a solid line. According to one American Indian myth, the jaguar got its spots by daubing mud on its body with its paws. Viewed closely, the markings on a jaguar's coat do look like paw prints.

The jaguar's underbelly is white and is marked with black splotches. The insides of the ears and

The rosettes on this jaguar's back are one of the markings that distinguish jaguars from leopards. Jaguars have larger rosettes than leopards do, and fewer of them.

legs as well as the lower muzzle, jaw, and throat are all white or pale gray. The jaguar's eyes have round pupils and irises with a golden or reddish-yellow color. Very young jaguar cubs have blue eyes.

The easiest way to distinguish a jaguar from a leopard, beside the jaguar's much more powerful build, is by the rosettes. The jaguar's rosettes are larger, fewer in number, and usually darker with thicker lines that enclose one or two small dots in the middle. Sometimes there are three dots. On the chest there are a series of black bars, which the leopard does not have. The jaguar's head is rounder than that of the leopard's, the jaguar has shorter, stockier limbs, and the jaguar's tail is shorter than the leopard's. It is tawny for two thirds of its length and white on its last third with solid black spots. This gives the tail's tip a ringed or barred look.

Coats of Different Colors

The jaguar's coloring and special markings give it a natural camouflage. This enables the jaguar to blend in perfectly with its forest surroundings. The big cat's black spots nearly disappear in the shadows as it moves through the forest. When it lies motionless in the dappled light that filters through the overhead trees, the jaguar can become almost invisible to its prey.

Some jaguars have a completely different appearance. Black, or melanistic, jaguars make up

▲ *Two big cats, two different colors: A melanistic, or black, jaguar and a spotted jaguar. The black coat of some jaguars is caused by a recessive genetic trait.*

about 6 percent of the jaguar population in parts of South America, especially in the Amazon region. The coats of melanistic jaguars are so dark that the big cat's black spots can be seen only dimly. Black jaguars are less common farther north. Native tribes believed that the black jaguars were a separate species from the spotted jaguars. Some still think that black jaguars are bigger and more ferocious than spotted jaguars. But scientists now know that the black color is a recessive genetic trait, like blue eyes in humans.

The northernmost melanistic jaguars can be found in the tropical evergreen forests of Chiapas in southern Mexico, and in Belize. These northern melanistic jaguars are somewhat lighter than the ones in South America. Their coats are a charcoal or dark chocolate instead of black. Black spots are easily visible on their coats. Yet another type of jaguar is white. This jaguar, the albino jaguar, has been observed in Paraguay, but it is extremely rare.

A Powerful Big Cat

The lion and the tiger are the only two big cats in the world that are larger than the jaguar. Theodore Roosevelt, our twenty-sixth president, who was an avid hunter and naturalist, described

Jaguar - Western Alliance for Nature - Microsoft Internet Explorer

File   Edit   View   Favorites   Tools   Help

Address http://www.wanconservancy.org/jaguar.htm

| Home Page | News & Views | Conservation Objectives | Nature Links | Wildlife Projects | What You Can Do... | About Us! |

Jaguar, the only large native carnivore entirely missing from the United States.

WAN Conservancy: Can We Bring Back the Jaguar? is a Web page of the Western Alliance for Nature Conservancy. This group has joined forces with the Northern Jaguar Project to safeguard Mexico's jaguars in hopes that these big cats will become reestablished in the United States.

the jaguar as "a big powerfully built creature, giving the same effect of strength that the tiger or lion does, and that the leopard and puma do not."[1]

When a person encounters a jaguar in the wild, the big cat often seems to be even larger than it actually is. This is especially true of the male jaguar. A combination of physical qualities is responsible for creating this impression of tremendous power. The jaguar's great head, thick barrel-shaped chest, heavyset body, short powerful limbs, and large paws can be intimidating. The jaguar is truly a very powerful animal for its size. A jaguar is capable of dragging an 800-pound (363-kilogram) bull 25 feet (8 meters) in its jaws and crushing the heaviest bones.

Measuring Up

Jaguars vary in length from about 5.3 to 6 feet (1.62 to 1.83 meters), excluding the tail. The largest jaguar ever measured was a giant cat in Brazil that was more than 9 feet (108 inches or 274 centimeters) long. The jaguar's tail, less than half the length of its head and body, measures between 17.0 and 29.5 inches (43 and 75 centimeters), compared to 23.5 to 39.5 inches (60 to 100 centimeters) for the leopard. Jaguars stand about 27 to 30 inches (68.6 to 76 centimeters) tall at the shoulders.

Jaguars weigh between 124 to 211 pounds (56 to 96 kilograms). But scientists have recorded

▲ *A jaguar's keen eyesight helps it find and catch prey.*

even larger jaguars that weigh as much as 288 to 333 pounds (131 to 151 kilograms). Female jaguars are typically about 20 percent smaller than males. Jaguars in southern Mexico and Central America are smaller than their South American cousins. The scientist Ernest Thompson Seton called them "dwarfs." These male jaguars usually weigh about 123 pounds (56 kilograms), and the females weigh about 90 pounds (41 kilograms). The jaguars farther north near the border between Mexico and the United States tend to be larger than those in southern Mexico.

▶ **Fierce Hunters**

Jaguars are also powerful, ferocious hunters. The jaguar has the strongest teeth and jaws of any

The strongest teeth of any American cat are bared by this roaring jaguar. It is also the only cat in the Americas that can roar.

http://www.cathouse-fcc.org/images/jagcubf2.jpg - Microsoft Internet Explorer

File   Edit   View   Favorites   Tools   Help

Address   http://www.cathouse-fcc.org/images/jagcubf2.jpg

A jaguar cub leaves little indication that it will grow up to be a strong and fierce predator. This image and others can be found on the **Jaguar** *(Panthera onca)* Web pages of the Feline Conservation Center site. The center includes a zoo that provides a home to wild cats.

American cat, including the mountain lion. Its muscular legs and shoulders give the jaguar the strength and agility to leap on its prey. It uses its razor-sharp front claws to grab and hold its prey while it crushes the skull with its powerful teeth and jaws. Like other cats, the jaguar can retract its claws when not using them.

The jaguar's senses also contribute to its success as a hunter. Since the jaguar mostly hunts in the dim light of dusk or dawn, it needs to have very sensitive eyes. The jaguar's eyes are set far apart, giving the big cat a wide field of vision. The pupils dilate widely to gather as much light as possible in the dark. As the jaguar walks silently through the dark forest, its excellent sense of vision allows it to spot prey that humans would have difficulty seeing.

The jaguar has a special layer of reflecting cells at the back of the eyes called the tapetum. Some of the light reaching the jaguar's eyes passes through the retina without being absorbed by the light-sensitive receptor cells. The tapetum layer at the back of the eyes acts like a mirror. It bounces the light back through the eyes so that even more light is absorbed. This almost doubles the sensitivity of the jaguar's eyes. The reflected light from the "mirror" at the back of the jaguar's eyes is the reason those eyes seem to shine in the beam of a lamp or the glow of a fire.

The jaguar's sharp sense of hearing alerts it to any prey in the vicinity. There are sensitive hairs in the jaguar's ears. These hairs can pick up the sound of an animal's movements even before the animal can be seen. Jaguars can also turn their ears in different directions to tell where a sound is coming from.

▶ A Voice in the Darkness

Unlike most cats, jaguars do not purr. However, the jaguar is the only cat in the Americas that can roar. One scientist described the sound as "a series of hoarse barking coughs, an interval of about one second separating each expiratory effort."[2] Many scientists regard the jaguar as a noisy animal whose voice is often heard at night. Several have described the jaguar's roar as a sequence of five or six guttural notes, something like "Uh, uh, uh, uh, uh, uh."[3] The sound carries far and could be a mating call or a kind of territorial marking. Jaguars also growl and mew on occasion and will snarl when cornered by dogs.

Life Stages

Scientists use the condition of the teeth, the degree of yellowing of the coat, and certain characteristics of the skull to determine a jaguar's age. They divide jaguars into five categories: cub, yearling, young mature, prime mature, and old. A cub is less than six months old. A yearling is six to eighteen months old. A young mature jaguar is eighteen months to three years old. A prime mature jaguar is three to eight years old. And an old jaguar is more than eight years old.

Jaguars usually live between fifteen and twenty years in the wild. Those in captivity, where conditions are less harsh and far less dangerous, may live up to twenty-five years. One jaguar was reported to have lived for thirty-two years.

Chapter 4 ▶

JAGUAR BEHAVIOR

The jaguar's scientific name, *Panthera onca*, describes the big cat's claws. *Panthera* is Latin for "hunter," and *onca* means "hook" or "barb." Those claws are essential in killing the prey jaguars feed on in their solitary hunts within their territories.

▶ A Jaguar's Home Range

A jaguar establishes its own home range, or territory, where other jaguars are not welcome. The jaguar will live alone within its range for most of the year. Home ranges vary greatly. A home range can be anywhere between 15 and 90 square miles (39 and 375.5 square kilometers). The size of the home range depends on the particular habitat, the availability of suitable prey, and the sex of the jaguar. Male jaguars usually have a range that is more than twice as big as the female jaguars' range, although the home ranges of males and females overlap. The males' territory may include the hunting grounds of several females.

In the beginning of the last century, Theodore Roosevelt described the territorial habits of

The size of a jaguar's home range depends upon several things, including the big cat's gender—males need a larger territory than females—and whether the land supports enough wildlife for the jaguar to eat.

jaguars in the southern Mato Grosso (literally "thick jungle") in Brazil. Roosevelt wrote: "In these marshes, each jaguar had a wide irregular range and travelled a good deal, perhaps only passing a day or two in a given locality, perhaps spending a week where game was plentiful."[1]

Jaguars mark their home ranges by placing scent marks. Charles Darwin observed another way in which jaguars mark their home range:

> One day, when hunting on the banks of the Uruguay, I was shown certain trees, to which these animals constantly recur for the purpose, as it is said, of sharpening their claws. I saw three well known trees; in front the bark was worn smooth as if by the breast of the animal, and on each side there were sharp scratches, or rather grooves, extending in an oblique line, nearly a yard in length. The scars were of different ages. A common method of ascertaining whether a jaguar is in the neighborhood is to examine these trees.[2]

Darwin later concluded that the tree scratching indicated the marking of a jaguar's home range.

▶ Solitary Wanderers

Jaguars tend to wander a great deal in search of prey. They have been seen, and sometimes killed, in areas that are far from their home range. While hunting prey, jaguars often travel across the lands lying between one natural habitat area and another. As noted by the American scientist E. W. Nelson,

Jaguars also mark their territory by making scratches in trees.

"Few predatory animals are such wanderers as the jaguar, which roams hundreds of miles from its original home, as shown by its occasional appearance within our borders."[3]

In 1955, Aldo Leopold reported an amazing story about a wandering jaguar that had been killed in Baja California, Mexico:

> I recently examined the tanned hide of a jaguar killed in September, 1955, near the southern tip of the Sierra Pedro Martir range, Baja California. This animal, an old male, must have wandered across the whole Sonoran Desert, crossed the Colorado River, and traveled south for 100 miles—a trip of at least 500 miles from regularly occupied jaguar range. Most vagrant jaguars are males, presumably driven from home in territorial disputes with other males. Once on the road, such vagrants seem to adopt travel as a way of life, like itinerant Englishmen.[4]

▷ Hunting and Killing Prey

Jaguars eat from 10 to 70 pounds (5 to 32 kilograms) of food daily. To satisfy such a healthy appetite, the jaguar needs to be an expert hunter. Its method of killing its prey differs from that of most cats. The lion, tiger, and leopard usually kill their prey by biting the neck or throat to suffocate or sever the spinal cord. But the jaguar uses its powerful jaws to deliver the fatal bite directly to the skull of its prey, crushing the skull and piercing the brain. The jaguar kills quickly by sinking its teeth through the thinnest part of the skull into the brain. This killing technique takes its toll on jaguars, though; they often break their teeth as they grow older.

Although the jaguar is an extremely powerful and ferocious hunter, it lives on mostly a diet of smaller prey. One swipe of the jaguar's powerful paw is enough to kill a small animal. But it will hunt whatever prey is available, large or small. The jaguar's diet consists of more than eighty-five species of animals. The diet includes capybaras,

A black jaguar on the prowl in South America. Jaguars have been known to travel long distances in search of food.

tapirs, peccaries, armadillos, caimans, iguanas, turtles, deer, otters, lizards, frogs, small rodents, birds, sloths, monkeys, and snakes, including the giant anaconda and boa constrictor.

In some places, peccaries are a major food item for jaguars. Peccaries are piglike creatures with razor-sharp tusks. They are found through-out most of the jaguar's range. Peccaries are fierce animals that travel in groups of up to one hundred or more. Jaguars keep their distance, waiting for the chance to pick off a straggler from the herd.

Stalking, Ambushing, Devouring

Most of the jaguar's hunting is done on the ground. The jaguar usually walks along a forest trail or beside a stream until it encounters prey. It normally walks with long strides of about twenty inches (fifty centimeters), often carrying its tail curved up. Then it will stalk or rush at the prey. The jaguar attacks that prey in a series of short, quick bounds. Jaguars can move very quickly. According to one observer, a jaguar can outdis-tance a horse over a short stretch, but the big cat will tire quickly. Sometimes the jaguar waits in ambush, its spotted coat making it invisible to passing prey as it lies in wait.

After killing small prey, the jaguar will eat the entire animal at once, including the skin and bones. When a jaguar kills larger prey, it will eat part of the animal. It stays in a crouching position, with its paws on the kill. The jaguar chews off piece after piece, with its head bent sideways. When it is finished eating, the jaguar will drag what is left of the animal to a hiding place in the nearest thicket. By doing so, the jaguar protects its kill from vultures or other animals that are scavengers.

People used to believe that the jaguar is nocturnal. After all, it does most of its hunting at dawn or dusk or during bright nights of moonshine or starlight. It rarely hunts during very dark nights. But the jaguar has also been observed hunting during the middle of the day.

Good Climbers

Jaguars are good climbers though not as agile as some smaller cats. However, a jaguar will sometimes climb the branches of a tree to go after a monkey, sloth, or a sleeping bird. Sometimes the jaguar will wait on a low-hanging branch for prey to pass beneath. Then it will drop from above, bringing the prey to the ground. Once a victim is dead, the jaguar will carry it off. The jaguar is so strong that it can drag an animal much larger than itself. One jaguar was reported to have hauled a full-grown horse for more than 200 feet (61 meters) and then carried it across a river.

▶ A Varied Diet

In the lowlands of Brazil and Venezuela, the jaguar feeds on capybara, the world's largest rodent. The capybara is a 100-pound (45-kilogram) semi-aquatic rodent that lives in herds along rivers, lakes, and streams. In the 1800s, J. R. Rengger watched a jaguar hunt a capybara and recorded his observations:

> Serpent-like the jaguar winds its way over the ground, often making a considerable detour to approach

Jaguars hunt in or near water much of the time. Unlike most cats, they are good swimmers.

from another direction where there is less risk of being detected. The capybara may get the stalker's wind when it is still far away and will rush into the water, uttering cries of alarm. Jaguars have been seen to jump into the river after a capybara and catch it before it could dive to safety.[5]

Feasting in Rivers

Much of the jaguar's hunting is done near or in the water. Like the tiger, the jaguar is one of the few cats that actually likes the water. Jaguars have

been seen playing about in the water. The jaguar is an excellent swimmer and can cross wide rivers. It swims with its head and the whole of its spine above the surface of the water. It paddles in almost a straight line when crossing a river. When the jaguar emerges from the water on the opposite shore, it looks around, shakes its body, and then shakes each paw separately.

Jaguars hunt caiman, South American cousins of the crocodile, in rivers. Another favorite food of the jaguar is the river turtle. The jaguar's teeth are powerful enough to

This jaguar seems ready for its fish dinner to arrive on the scene. The big cats have been known to use their massive paws to knock fish out of the water and onto a riverbank.

San Diego
Zoo's Animal
Bytes: Jaguar

San Diego Zoo's Animal Bytes: Jaguar - Microsoft Internet Explorer

File   Edit   View   Favorites   Tools   Help

Address | http://www.sandiegozoo.org/animalbytes/t-jaguar.html

SAN DIEGO ZOO.org

| animal bytes home | reptiles | birds | insects & spiders | mammals | amphibians |

Quick facts
▶ Video Byte: Jaguar

📷 Photo Bytes

Class: Mammalia (Mammals)
Order: Carnivora
Family: Felidae
Genus: Panthera
Species: onca
Length: 3.8 to 6 feet (1.1 to 1.8 meters); tail length 18 to 30

Mammals: Jaguar

Range: North America, Central America, and South America
Habitat: rain forests, swampy areas, grasslands, woodlands, dry forests, and even deserts

Is that a jaguar I'm looking at?
While jaguars and leopards look a lot alike, there are ways to tell them apart. Jaguars are stockier and heavier, with shorter, thicker tails. They have dark spots on their backs, called rosettes, with an irregular broken border and often a spot in the center. Leopards (from Africa and Asia) also have dark rosettes on a tawny coat, but if you look closely at each rosette, you'll see that there is no spot inside, and the rosette edge is unbroken.

A roaring good time
There are four big cats in the biological grouping called *Panthera*: jaguars, lions, tigers, and leopards. These are the only big cats that can roar. They roar to scare off other animals and defend their territory.

What's a black panther?
Most jaguars have tawny-colored fur with black rosettes, but

This San Diego Zoo Web site offers an overview of the jaguar. Learn about jaguars and find additional information about the efforts to save this endangered cat.

Access this Web site from http://www.myreportlinks.com

tear through the tough armor of the turtle's shell. While exploring the South American rain forests, American naturalist Leo E. Miller witnessed the big cats' taste for turtle eggs: "The hoarse cough of jaguars was heard almost nightly; it was the season when great numbers of turtles left the river at nightfall to deposit their eggs in the sandbanks, and the jaguars left the forest at dark to dig up and feed on these eggs."[6]

Jaguars also eat some fish that they catch in the rivers. J. R. Rengger observed a jaguar fishing in a river in Paraguay:

> It [the jaguar] was sitting crouched on a spit of land, where the water was running rather more

swiftly, the kind of place favored by a predatory fish known in Paraguay as "dorado." Occasionally it bent forward, its eyes fixed on the surface of the river as if it wished to penetrate the depth below.

After about a quarter of an hour, I saw it slap the water with its paw and throw a large fish on to the bank. It was fishing in exactly the same way as our domestic cat.[7]

In the Amazon and Guiana forests, jaguars will enter shallow pools in order to catch the large fish known as pirarucu, or arapaima. This fish can reach a length of up to 13 feet (4 meters) and a weight of 450 pounds (204 kilograms). The American Indians of the Amazon, according to one writer, say that "the jaguar comes at night and crouches on a log or branch over the water; he raps the surface with his tail, gently, and the 'tambakis' or other fruit-eating fish, come to the sound, when he knocks them out with his paw."[8]

▶ Lack of Prey Leads to Fear and Hate

In some places, though, jaguars kill domesticated animals, such as cattle, horses, and dogs. This usually happens on ranches that were once wild lands and the natural home of the jaguar and other wild animals. In many places, jungles have been cleared to provide grazing for livestock. The jaguars in these areas are not only losing habitat but are also now deprived of their native prey. Without other food sources, jaguars sometimes

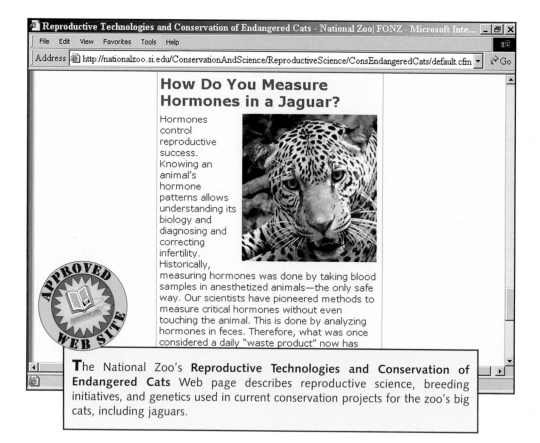

Reproductive Technologies and Conservation of Endangered Cats - National Zoo| FONZ - Microsoft Inte...

File   Edit   View   Favorites   Tools   Help

Address http://nationalzoo.si.edu/ConservationAndScience/ReproductiveScience/ConsEndangeredCats/default.cfm ⌖ Go

How Do You Measure Hormones in a Jaguar?

Hormones control reproductive success. Knowing an animal's hormone patterns allows understanding its biology and diagnosing and correcting infertility. Historically, measuring hormones was done by taking blood samples in anesthetized animals—the only safe way. Our scientists have pioneered methods to measure critical hormones without even touching the animal. This is done by analyzing hormones in feces. Therefore, what was once considered a daily "waste product" now has

The National Zoo's **Reproductive Technologies and Conservation of Endangered Cats** Web page describes reproductive science, breeding initiatives, and genetics used in current conservation projects for the zoo's big cats, including jaguars.

kill cattle because the only alternative is starvation. Farmers and ranchers kill jaguars on sight to protect their livestock. But recent studies by groups involved in jaguar conservation have shown that where enough natural prey exists, jaguars and livestock can coexist.

The killing of humans by jaguars, though rare, has happened. In its wilderness habitat, the jaguar tends to shy away from people. But in places where the big cat has gotten used to the presence of humans, it may sometimes act aggressively.

This might happen along big rivers with heavy boat traffic. But although jaguars have killed individuals, there is no known case of a jaguar hunting humans for food in the way that lions, tigers, and leopards sometimes do.

As Edward W. Nelson, who studied wild animals in Mexico, notes:

> During the years I spent in its country, mainly in the open, I made careful inquiry without hearing of a single case where one [a jaguar] had attacked human beings. So far as I could learn, it had practically the same shy and cowardly nature as the mountain lion. Despite this, the natives throughout its tropical home have a great fear of el tigre, as I saw evidence repeatedly in Mexico. Apparently this fear is based wholly on its strength and potential ability to harm man if it so desires.[9]

Jaguar Reproduction

The solitary jaguar seeks company only when it is time to mate. Male and female jaguars may stay together for up to four or five weeks or as long as the female is in estrus, or heat. A mated pair will eat together but will not hunt together.

The female jaguar becomes sexually mature between two and three years of age. The male jaguar takes longer, reaching maturity between the ages of three and four years. Jaguars do not have a defined breeding season and can mate at any time of the year, but they seem to follow a pattern of reproducing depending on where they live.

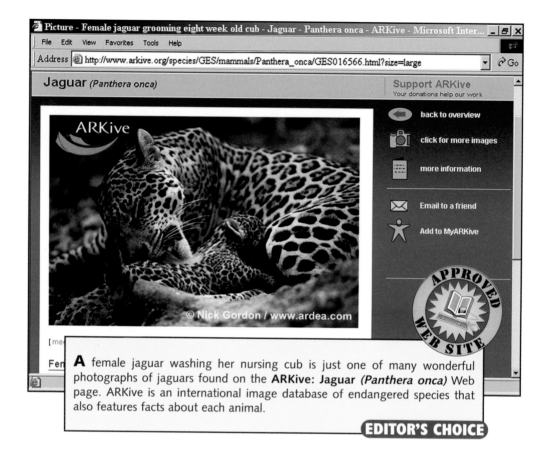

Picture - Female jaguar grooming eight week old cub - Jaguar - Panthera onca - ARKive - Microsoft Inter...

File   Edit   View   Favorites   Tools   Help

Address   http://www.arkive.org/species/GES/mammals/Panthera_onca/GES016566.html?size=large   Go

Jaguar *(Panthera onca)*

Support ARKive
Your donations help our work

back to overview

click for more images

more information

Email to a friend

Add to MyARKive

ARKive

© Nick Gordon / www.ardea.com

A female jaguar washing her nursing cub is just one of many wonderful photographs of jaguars found on the **ARKive: Jaguar *(Panthera onca)*** Web page. ARKive is an international image database of endangered species that also features facts about each animal.

EDITOR'S CHOICE

In areas with distinct seasons, mating seems to be timed so that the births will occur during the rainy season. That is when food and water are most available. In Belize, the mating season occurs between the drier months from February to May, so that most jaguar births there occur between June and August, during the rainy season. In northern Mexico, mating usually takes place in midwinter to early spring. Meanwhile, in Paraguay, much farther south, the mating season is in August and September.

The best time to hear the roar of the jaguar is during mating season. Sometimes, more than one male jaguar at a time will pursue a female, leading to fights between the males. One jaguar quickly asserts his dominance over the others. The dominant male gets to mate with the female, and the weaker males slink away.

The gestation period, the time in which the female carries her young before it is born, usually lasts about three months, varying from about ninety-three to 105 days. Before giving birth, the female jaguar seeks out a secluded site for a den. She may choose a natural cave, a spot beneath an overhanging rock, a dense thicket, or even an abandoned mine. The jaguar's litter usually consists of two cubs but there may be as many as four cubs and as few as one.

From Cub to Youngster

Jaguar cubs weigh between 30.0 and 30.5 ounces (850 and 865 grams) when they are first born. They measure just less than 16 inches (41 centimeters) in length. At birth, the cubs are blind. They open their eyes, which are blue, for the first time between three and thirteen days later. Their coats are buff colored with large black spots. A jaguar mother hardly leaves the den during the first few days after giving birth. She keeps the den clean by eating whatever waste products the cubs

These young jaguar twins do not need to fend for themselves, since they are zoo residents.

make. If anything in the area disturbs the mother, she will carry her cubs to a new shelter.

By six weeks of age, the cubs begin following their mother around outside the den, but they remain hidden for safety while the mother hunts. By age ten to eleven weeks, the cubs begin eating meat, which their mother brings to them in pieces. Most young cubs are weaned after twenty-two weeks, but some continue to nurse until they are six months old.

By the age of seven months, jaguar cubs have coats that resemble those of their parents. In two more months, the cubs are almost half grown. While mothers are most responsible for raising their young, fathers sometimes take an interest in the cubs. Scientists have occasionally reported male jaguars bringing food for their cubs. Female jaguars, however, do not allow the father into the den. When the cubs are small, the mother senses that her young need to be protected from their father.

Young jaguars learn how to hunt by watching their mother. They stay with her until they are one and a half to two years old. By this time, their milk teeth (baby teeth) have been replaced by permanent teeth. Now the young jaguars are forced to go off and fend for themselves. Sometimes a young female will be allowed to share part of her mother's home range. Young males, however, usually have to establish a new territory for themselves.

THE JAGUAR IN HUMAN CULTURES

The jaguar has played an important part in the lives of humans for more than ten thousand years. In some of the oldest cultures of the Americas, people believed the jaguar possessed great powers, and some worshipped the big cat as a representative of the gods on earth.

What exactly is a representative of the gods? To these early inhabitants of Mexico, Central America, and South America, the jaguar was more than an animal but less than a god. In his study of jaguars, Dr. Alan Rabinowitz wondered about the historic role of this big cat:

> Where did jaguars fit in? They were not considered gods, nor were they thought to be simply powerful animals that shared the earth with man. It seemed as though, to the ancient Maya, they were living symbols of the gods and their power. They were creatures of the night, and allied with the underworld. They were of man's world, yet not of man's world. They were real, yet not real. They were definable by the senses, yet they represented all that was unknown and mysterious in the jungle. How to categorize their role? Perhaps they

were less understood by the people than the gods themselves. We shall never know. [1]

The Jaguar in Amazonia

The Tucaño Indians of the Amazon believed the jaguar was created by the sun god to be his representative on earth. The sun gave the jaguar a yellow coat, signifying the sun's power, and the voice of thunder, believed to be the voice of God.[2] Modern Tucaño Indians still believe in the power of the jaguar. They hear the roar of thunder in the jaguar's roar, announcing the approach of rain.

Other people in these lands believe the jaguar represents the god of darkness. They think the

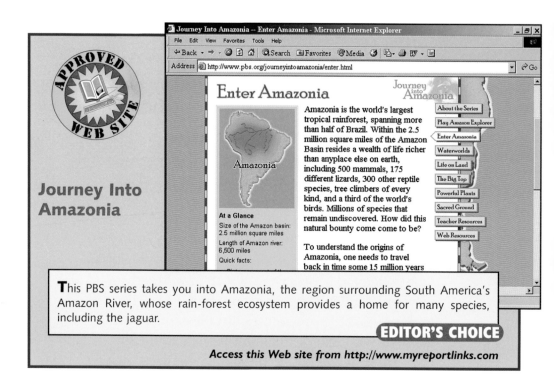

Journey Into Amazonia

Enter Amazonia

Journey into Amazonia

Amazonia is the world's largest tropical rainforest, spanning more than half of Brazil. Within the 2.5 million square miles of the Amazon Basin resides a wealth of life richer than anyplace else on earth, including 500 mammals, 175 different lizards, 300 other reptile species, tree climbers of every kind, and a third of the world's birds. Millions of species that remain undiscovered. How did this natural bounty come to be?

To understand the origins of Amazonia, one needs to travel back in time some 15 million years

At a Glance
Size of the Amazon basin: 2.5 million square miles
Length of Amazon river: 6,500 miles
Quick facts:

About the Series
Play Amazon Explorer
Enter Amazonia
Waterworlds
Life on Land
The Big Top
Powerful Plants
Sacred Ground
Teacher Resources
Web Resources

This PBS series takes you into Amazonia, the region surrounding South America's Amazon River, whose rain-forest ecosystem provides a home for many species, including the jaguar.

EDITOR'S CHOICE

Access this Web site from http://www.myreportlinks.com

jaguar causes eclipses to occur by swallowing the sun. During an eclipse, some tribes follow a traditional custom of howling and shouting to scare off the jaguar.

To this day, shamans among the tribes of Amazonia, the region in northern South America surrounding the Amazon River that makes up the world's largest tropical rain forest, wear jaguar costumes in ceremonies. These healers and spiritual leaders don ceremonial outfits complete with headdresses made of upturned jaguar claws and necklaces of jaguar teeth. They also paint black spots on their faces to imitate the big cat's coloring.

▶ "Becoming" Jaguars

Following ancient traditions, the shamans transform themselves into jaguars to tap into the power of the animal. To "become" a jaguar, the shaman drinks jaguar blood, eats raw meat, and sleeps on the ground. He also eats certain plants that are hallucinogenics (substances that cause hallucinations), supposedly enabling him to see, hear, and smell with the heightened senses of the jaguar. In this way, the shaman is said to borrow, for a time, the jaguar's powers. These powers can be used by the shaman for good or to harm, to cure a person of a disease or to take revenge on an enemy.

Elsewhere in South America, the jaguar played an important role in the mythology of many early

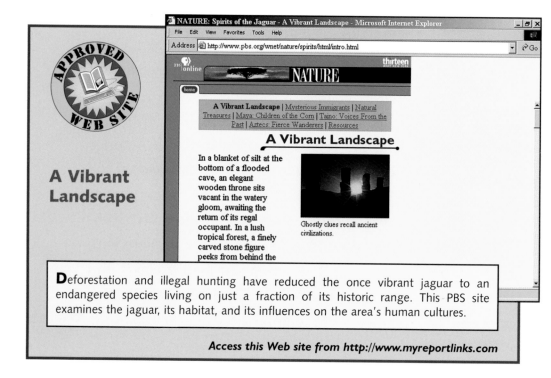

NATURE: Spirits of the Jaguar - A Vibrant Landscape - Microsoft Internet Explorer

File   Edit   View   Favorites   Tools   Help

Address   http://www.pbs.org/wnet/nature/spirits/html/intro.html

NATURE

thirteen

home

A Vibrant Landscape | Mysterious Immigrants | Natural Treasures | Maya: Children of the Corn | Taino: Voices From the Past | Aztecs: Fierce Wanderers | Resources

A Vibrant Landscape

A Vibrant Landscape

In a blanket of silt at the bottom of a flooded cave, an elegant wooden throne sits vacant in the watery gloom, awaiting the return of its regal occupant. In a lush tropical forest, a finely carved stone figure peeks from behind the

Ghostly clues recall ancient civilizations.

Deforestation and illegal hunting have reduced the once vibrant jaguar to an endangered species living on just a fraction of its historic range. This PBS site examines the jaguar, its habitat, and its influences on the area's human cultures.

Access this Web site from http://www.myreportlinks.com

cultures, including those of the highlands of the Andes Mountains. Some early cultures that pre-date the Inca worshipped cat gods. They depicted them with carved and painted heads that seem to represent jaguars. Pottery vessels from the Inca civilization in Peru depict jaguars eating their victims. A one-thousand-year-old Peruvian tapestry shows a full-face jaguar head. Alongside the head are two standing jaguars.

▶ **The Olmec**

Along Mexico's Gulf Coast, in what are today the Mexican states of Veracruz and Tabasco, the

Olmec built the first-known civilization of Mexico and Central America. Olmec society, which flourished from 1200 B.C. to 400 B.C., included a small elite upper class of priests and nobles. These leaders ruled a much larger class of peasant farmers.

At sites such as San Lorenzo and La Venta, the Olmec built pyramids, buildings with courtyards, and huge stone monuments including columns, altars, and gigantic heads. Some of the stone heads weigh as much as 44 tons (40 metric tons). Each head is carved in the round from a single

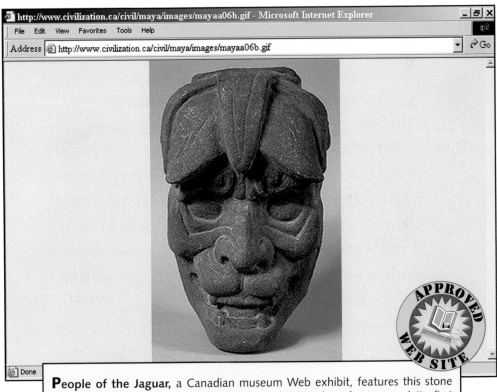

http://www.civilization.ca/civil/maya/images/mayaa06b.gif - Microsoft Internet Explorer

File   Edit   View   Favorites   Tools   Help

Address http://www.civilization.ca/civil/maya/images/mayaa06b.gif   Go

Done

People of the Jaguar, a Canadian museum Web exhibit, features this stone mask from around 900 B.C. of a jaguar god. This idea of a jaguar deity first appeared in the Olmec civilization as a were-jaguar.

block of basalt, a dark gray to black rock. The largest one is more than 9 feet (2.7 meters) tall. In addition to stone heads depicting humans, the Olmec also carved huge 20-ton (18-metric ton) stone heads of jaguars. Archaeologists believe that Olmec workers moved the stone sculptures over land on rolling logs. The giant heads were then transferred to rafts and moved along waterways to different sites.

The Were-Jaguar

An important part of Olmec mythology is based on a mother goddess mating with a jaguar. Their union brought forth a strange half-human, half-jaguar creature known as a were-jaguar. To the Olmec, the jaguar may have represented a power-ful rain god or perhaps the earth, maize, or fertility. The Olmec used jaguar masks and capes to ornament the costumes of warriors, nobles, and priests. Olmec priests communicated with the spirit of the jaguar, which visited them in their dreams. Olmec religious rites included human sac-rifice along with the sacrificing of jaguars and other animals.

The largest Olmec structure we know of is the ceremonial House of the Jaguar, which shows the tremendous importance of the jaguar in the Olmec culture. The Olmec carved thousands of were-jaguars out of jade. They also made jaguar figures out of terra-cotta and stone. Jaguars also appear in Olmec cave paintings, and a stylized jaguar is the subject of an Olmec floor mosaic.

The Olmec civilization disappeared by 400 B.C., perhaps destroyed by outside invaders. Nobody knows for sure, since the Olmec left no written records. But Olmec culture influenced the other major civilizations that followed in Mexico and Central America. Cities of later civilizations followed the Olmec pattern of combining pyramids, plazas, and monumental sculpture. And the jaguar continued to represent a symbol of awesome power for the other cultures, appearing in their pottery and sculpture.

The Zapotec

The Zapotec, whose civilization flourished from about 1000 B.C. to A.D. 700, lived in the Oaxaca Valley, where the present-day Mexican state of Oaxaca is. These people built the city of San José Mogote around 1000 B.C. and erected stone platforms, temples, and monumental sculptures. The Zapotec replaced their original rain god, Cocijo, with a man-eating jaguar that was depicted in both human and animal form.

By 500 B.C., the Zapotec had developed a calendar system based on movements of the sun. They also invented a hieroglyphic writing system. Around this time, they built the city of Monte Albán

A double-sided jaguar serves as a Mayan altar. The animal was revered by many of the ancient native cultures of Mexico and Central America.

on a mountaintop overlooking the Oaxaca valley. The earliest dated writing in the Americas, from around 500 B.C., is found on carved stone slabs at Monte Albán.[3] There, jaguars are depicted in murals, on pottery vessels, as clay figurines, and as masks. Almost all of these jaguar images are either some combination of a jaguar and another animal or a human in a jaguar costume. Even the depictions that most closely resemble jaguars include elements of other creatures, such as feathers or birdlike eyes. Some are spotted with flowers or seashells rather than rosettes.

At Dainzú, another Zapotec site in Oaxaca, the entrance to a tomb has been carved in the image of a jaguar. By A.D. 600, the Zapotec civilization began to decline, although again, archaeologists are not sure of the reason.

▶ The Maya

The Maya civilization, which lasted from about 200 B.C. to about A.D. 900, flourished in Mexico's Yucatán Peninsula and extended into northern Guatemala. Great Maya cities and settlements included Tikal, Palenque, Copán, Uxmal, and Chichén Itzá, home to temples, palaces, and elaborate stone carvings. In the center of each city were tall pyramids that towered over the surrounding jungle. Surrounding each busy city

One World Journeys | Jaguar: Lord of the Mayan Jungle - Microsoft Internet Explorer

File   Edit   View   Favorites   Tools   Help

Address   http://www.oneworldjourneys.com/expeditions/jaguar/   Go

fusionsparkmedia

JAGUAR
Lord of the Mayan Jungle

Searching for the Jaguar
Scientists hunt the jaguar to ensure its survival

Join the Expedition Now
▶ English   ▶ Español   ▶ 日本語版

Follow scientists and hounds as they crash through a Mexican rainforest chasing the fleeting shadow of the jaguar. The survival of the rainforest and the jaguar depends on this hunt and the answers it provides. Even while many fight to save the jaguar, its populat... territor...

Note: This Expedition requires Macromedia's Flash 4 player and Apple's QuickTime player.

Join us

APPROVED WEB SITE

Jaguar: Lord of the Mayan Jungle

One World Journeys, virtual tours presented by a group of journalists, takes viewers to interesting places around the world. At this site, journey to the land of the Maya, home of jaguars.

Access this Web site from http://www.myreportlinks.com

center were residential districts with populations in the tens of thousands.

Each Maya city, ruled by a god-king, also served as a religious ceremonial center. The Maya believed in many gods, each associated with a different part of the natural world. To please the gods and make sure they kept the world in balance, the Maya practiced human sacrifice. The victims were usually enemy prisoners who had been captured in battle.

The Maya shared the Olmec's fascination with jaguars. To the Maya, the big cat symbolized power, strength, and bravery. In fact, the Maya term for going to war translates as "spreading the jaguar skin." They raised jaguars in captivity to ensure an adequate supply for sacrifice, because they sometimes sacrificed the big cats.

The Maya believed that jaguars were a link between the world of the living and the world of the dead. In Maya belief, Kinich Ahau, their sun god, transformed himself into a jaguar during his nightly journey through the underworld. Maya priests dressed in the skins of jaguars. Twins in the Maya creation myth, Hunahpú and Xbalanque, are depicted in Maya art with jaguar markings. Hunahpú has large black spots on his cheeks and body. Xbalanque has jaguar skin patches around his mouth and on his body and limbs.

"Ghost Cat"

This *Audubon* article examines a lawsuit by the Center for Biological Diversity against the U.S. Fish and Wildlife Service for refusing to designate critical habitat for jaguars in the United States.

Access this Web site from http://www.myreportlinks.com

The Temple of the Jaguars at Chichén Itzá.

The Maya carved statues of jaguars and built jaguar temples in their sacred cities. At Chichén Itzá, the Temple of Kukulcán, a great pyramid also known as El Castillo, features a jaguar throne carved out of a huge block of limestone. The throne is studded with seventy-three jade spots, representing the spots of the jaguar. Chichén Itzá is also home to the Temple of the Jaguars, which contains many carvings of this creature so important to the Maya civilization.

Their religious beliefs led the Maya to devise a calendar, and their achievements in mathematics and astronomy were far ahead of their time. The Maya also developed the most advanced writing system in the ancient Americas. It consisted of about eight hundred hieroglyphic symbols, or glyphs.

▶ Teotihuacán

The Teotihuacán civilization in the Valley of Mexico arose around the same time as the Maya civilization. The people of Teotihuacán were drawn to the area by its fertile soil and abundant resources. During the first century A.D., they began building the city of Teotihuacán, outside what is today Mexico City, Mexico's capital. At its height, during the 400s, Teotihuacán may have had a population greater than 125,000. It was certainly one of the largest cities in the world at the time and

Tezcatlipoca, a god who could take the form of a jaguar, was revered by the Toltec and later by the Aztec, a warlike people who conquered the Toltec.

featured six hundred pyramids, two thousand apartment complexes, and a great market compound. The giant Pyramid of the Sun in the center of the city was larger at its base than Egypt's Great Pyramid.

Like the Olmec, Zapotec, and Maya, the people of Teotihuacán were fascinated with jaguars. Jaguars did not live in the area, however, so they were raised in captivity. The remains of jaguars and their droppings have been found in cages beneath the Temple of the Moon in Teotihuacán.

▶ The Toltec

As the Maya were disappearing into the jungles of the Yucatán, a new empire arose in the Valley of Mexico. The warlike Toltec conquered the various peoples of the Valley of Mexico around A.D. 900. They ruled their empire from their capital at Tula, in what is now the Mexican state of Hidalgo. The Toltec built pyramids and temples and carved tall pillars in the shape of fierce warriors.

Although the Toltec worshipped Tezcatlipoca, a god of war, and Quetzalcoatl, a god of peace (a feathered serpent, part quetzal bird and part snake), they also revived the old were-jaguar and jaguar symbols of the Olmec to symbolize power. In their art, the Toltec depicted jaguars eating the hearts of their enemies and prisoners. A popular theme at Tula was the pairing of jaguars and

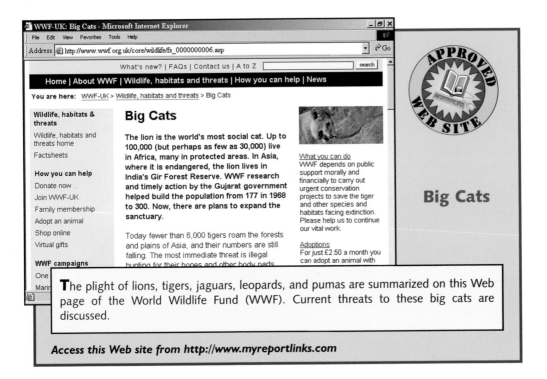

WWF-UK: Big Cats - Microsoft Internet Explorer

File   Edit   View   Favorites   Tools   Help

Address http://www.wwf.org.uk/core/wildlife/fs_0000000006.asp   Go

What's new? | FAQs | Contact us | A to Z   search

Home | About WWF | Wildlife, habitats and threats | How you can help | News

You are here: WWF-UK > Wildlife, habitats and threats > Big Cats

Wildlife, habitats & threats

Wildlife, habitats and threats home

Factsheets

How you can help

Donate now

Join WWF-UK

Family membership

Adopt an animal

Shop online

Virtual gifts

WWF campaigns

One

Mari

Big Cats

The lion is the world's most social cat. Up to 100,000 (but perhaps as few as 30,000) live in Africa, many in protected areas. In Asia, where it is endangered, the lion lives in India's Gir Forest Reserve. WWF research and timely action by the Gujarat government helped build the population from 177 in 1968 to 300. Now, there are plans to expand the sanctuary.

Today fewer than 6,000 tigers roam the forests and plains of Asia, and their numbers are still falling. The most immediate threat is illegal hunting for their bones and other body parts

What you can do
WWF depends on public support morally and financially to carry out urgent conservation projects to save the tiger and other species and habitats facing extinction. Please help us to continue our vital work.

Adoptions
For just £2.50 a month you can adopt an animal with

Big Cats

APPROVED WEB SITE

The plight of lions, tigers, jaguars, leopards, and pumas are summarized on this Web page of the World Wildlife Fund (WWF). Current threats to these big cats are discussed.

Access this Web site from http://www.myreportlinks.com

eagles, twin symbols of warfare. The Toltec ruled the area until about A.D. 1200, when they were conquered by a warlike nomadic people from the deserts of northern Mexico.

▷ The Aztec

Those northern warriors, the Aztec, set out to build the most powerful empire yet known in Mexico and Central America. According to Aztec legend, they were guided by the vision of an eagle, the symbol of their war god, that was perched on a cactus while devouring a serpent—Quetazlcoatl.

In 1325, the Aztec founded the city of Tenochtitlán. (Present-day Mexico City is built on

The Temple of the Great Jaguar in Tikal, built by the Maya.

the ruins of Tenochtitlán.) The Aztec built their great city on an island in the middle of Lake Tezcoco in the Valley of Mexico. They then built three causeways, or raised roads, over the water and marshland to connect Tenochtitlán to the mainland.

Aztec society consisted of many classes—the priesthood, the nobility, the military, merchants, commoners, and slaves. Military leaders held great power because the Aztec engaged in constant warfare.

The Ruler of All Animals

Like many other cultures of the region, the Aztec admired the jaguar, considering it the ruler of all animals. To the Aztec, the jaguar was the bravest, wisest, and fiercest of them all. Called Ocelotl by the Aztec, the jaguar was used to symbolize warriors and rulers. The Aztec emperors wore jaguar capes and furnished their palace with jaguar hide thrones, mats, and cushions. The bravest Aztec warriors belonged to one of two elite military orders, the Jaguar Knights and the Eagle Knights. Dressed in jaguar or eagle costumes, these warriors had the honor of protecting the emperor. Each year, at the end of the summer, the Jaguar Knights and the Eagle Knights paraded in an annual military display. The Jaguar Knights wore a jaguar skin with the jaguar head used as a helmet.

▷ A Vast Empire

By around 1500, Tenochtitlán was larger than any European capital of the time. By conquering other groups, the Aztec controlled a vast empire of perhaps 15 million people that reached from central Mexico to the Atlantic and Pacific coasts and south into Oaxaca. Conquered peoples were forced to pay tribute to the Aztec and also furnish them with a steady supply of people to serve as slaves or for human sacrifice.

The Aztec adopted many of their gods and religious beliefs from the Toltec, including Tezcatlipoca and Quetzalcoatl. According to Aztec myths, Tezcatlipoca was knocked from the sky by Quetzalcoatl, the feathered serpent. Tezcatlipoca fell into the sea and was changed into the Great Jaguar.

Tezcatlipoca was the Aztec's god of the night, who appeared in the form of a jaguar. He must have been important to the Aztec priests, who

The great religious symbolism of the jaguar subsided with the Spanish conquest of the Americas, but the big cat's power and majesty are still revered—and sometimes feared—by many descendants of the Olmec, Maya, and Aztec peoples.

used the claws, skins, and hearts of jaguars in their rituals. Inside the Great Temple in Tenochtitlán was a huge sculpture of a jaguar with a hollowed-out back. The priests placed sacrificial human hearts inside it.

Another Aztec ceremonial site known as Malinalco was carved out of a limestone hillside. Inside is a room containing sculptures of jaguars and eagles. Along a

A drawing of an Aztec jaguar warrior, bearing a shield and sword and wearing the skin of one of the big cats. This image is from the Codex Magliabechiano, created during the early Spanish colonial period, in the mid-1500s.

stairway leading to the room are stone jaguars cut from the same limestone of the hillside. The room served as a meeting hall for the Jaguar Knights and Eagle Knights. The site, a "warrior house," came under the protection of a special god.[4]

The Effects of the Spanish Conquest

Although it seems hard to believe, the Aztec Empire, which had taken hundreds of years to build, was crushed between 1519 and 1521. How did this happen? When the Spanish conquistador Hernán Cortés arrived in Tenochtitlán, with a relatively small army of six hundred soldiers, he managed to defeat the Aztec emperor Montezuma and his powerful armies.

With the Spanish conquest of Mexico and Central and South America, the great religious and symbolic worship of the jaguar came to an end. Jaguar imagery, however, continued to appear in different forms in many cultures throughout Mexico, including the Tarascan, Huichol, and Huasteca cultures. It also spread as far north as the American Southwest, where the jaguar once roamed.

Jaguar Imagery in the American Southwest

Many cultures in the American Southwest appear to have been influenced by the civilizations of

Mexico. Petroglyphs of catlike animals on canyon walls in New Mexico are similar to the portrayals of jaguars by Mexican cultures to the south.

The Mimbres culture of New Mexico and Arizona, which flourished from A.D. 1000 to 1250, made pottery bearing realistic images of animals. The images of cats on their pottery were most likely jaguars because of the striped tails and the abstract designs that fill the bodies. A mural on the wall of a kiva at Broken Pottery Ruin, New Mexico, clearly depicts jaguars, with their spots and striped tails. (Kivas are Pueblo Indian ceremonial structures, usually round and often built underground.) Cat images also appear in Pueblo kivas in Arizona.

Enduring Symbolism

The jaguar's striking image continues to be a powerful symbol for many people. Twentieth-century Mexican artist Rufino Tamayo painted a mural depicting the Feathered Serpent (representing daylight and enlightenment) battling a jaguar (representing darkness and evil). The mural is displayed at the National Museum of Anthropology in Mexico City. Elsewhere in that city, a mural by the Mexican painter Diego Rivera shows Spaniards lancing a jaguar. In that painting, the jaguar represents the peoples of Mexico, who suffered under Spanish conquest.

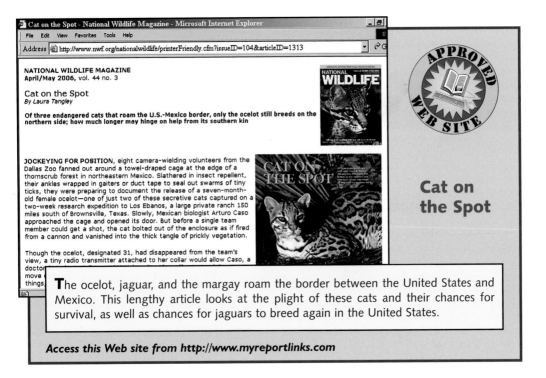

NATIONAL WILDLIFE MAGAZINE
April/May 2006, vol. 44 no. 3

Cat on the Spot
By Laura Tangley

Of three endangered cats that roam the U.S.-Mexico border, only the ocelot still breeds on the northern side; how much longer may hinge on help from its southern kin

JOCKEYING FOR POSITION, eight camera-wielding volunteers from the Dallas Zoo fanned out around a towel-draped cage at the edge of a thornscrub forest in northeastern Mexico. Slathered in insect repellent, their ankles wrapped in gaiters or duct tape to seal out swarms of tiny ticks, they were preparing to document the release of a seven-month-old female ocelot—one of just two of these secretive cats captured on a two-week research expedition to Los Ebanos, a large private ranch 150 miles south of Brownsville, Texas. Slowly, Mexican biologist Arturo Caso approached the cage and opened its door. But before a single team member could get a shot, the cat bolted out of the enclosure as if fired from a cannon and vanished into the thick tangle of prickly vegetation.

Though the ocelot, designated 31, had disappeared from the team's view, a tiny radio transmitter attached to her collar would allow Caso, a doctor...

Cat on the Spot

The ocelot, jaguar, and the margay roam the border between the United States and Mexico. This lengthy article looks at the plight of these cats and their chances for survival, as well as chances for jaguars to breed again in the United States.

Access this Web site from http://www.myreportlinks.com

Today, perhaps the most famous image of a jaguar is the sleek jaguar hood ornament on the luxury sports cars and sedans made by Jaguar. The Jacksonville Jaguars of the National Football League have also capitalized on the image of these powerful cats, and high school and college teams have followed suit. Video games and computers have borrowed the name to represent some of their products. Somehow, the powerful symbol of the jaguar has made the transition from the spirit world of the shamans and their gods to today's materialistic world. Despite the enduring popularity of this animal for what it symbolizes, however, it is still in danger of disappearing from the earth forever.

THREATS TO THE CATS' SURVIVAL

Jaguars have only one predator, but it is the most dangerous predator on earth—the human being. For a long time, jaguars have suffered severely at the hands of humans, whether for ceremonial use, as with the Maya and Aztec, or a strictly material one, such as humankind's desire to wear the skins or fur of wild animals. The jaguar's beautiful markings have made it highly prized by people. The trade in jaguar pelts has resulted in many of the big cats losing their lives.

This report from 1883 gives an example of how valuable jaguar fur was in the early days of the settlement of Arizona:

> The leopard [jaguar] . . . is a more compact built animal than the lion [mountain lion], and fully as heavy. The Papago and Yaqui Indians say he is much more to be feared than the lion. He is beautifully marked, and his skin commands a high price, both here and in Sonora, being in demand among the Mexican vaqueros [cowboys] for leggings and saddle trimmings.[1]

In more recent years, the jaguar paid a heavy price for its beautiful skin. By the 1940s, there were relatively few tigers and leopards still around after they had been hunted almost to extinction. So hunters turned to the jaguar. By the late 1960s, about fifteen thousand jaguars were being shot each year just in the Amazon jungles of Brazil. Trade in jaguar skins brought in nearly $30 million per year. In 1968, more than seven thousand

The beautiful spotted coat of the jaguar has long made it a favorite target for hunters, who sell the big cats' pelts for a lot of money.

jaguar skins worth more than $750,000 were imported to the United States.

Thankfully, the widespread killing of jaguars for their skins has long since ended. But even though international laws now exist to protect jaguars, each of the countries where the jaguar lives also has its own laws, making it difficult to protect the species throughout its range. Jaguar conservation is made even more difficult because scientists also do not yet have a good estimate of how many jaguars remain in the wild.

▶ Illegal Killing

The jaguar was considered an endangered species by the government of the United States in 1973 when it was listed under the Endangered Species Act. That law protected jaguars within the borders of the United States but had no authority in the other countries where jaguars live. The same year, however, jaguars were listed as an Appendix I species in CITES, the international agreement that prohibits trade in animals that could affect their survival.

Because the jaguar is an endangered species, it is illegal under CITES to trade the jaguar's skin or any other part of the jaguar for commercial gain. But despite the legal protections granted to jaguars, illegal killing of jaguars continues in many places. The countries that participate in

Jaguar conservation is made more difficult because these big cats are so elusive. Researchers are still trying to get a good estimate of how many jaguars there actually are throughout their range.

CITES do so voluntarily. The limits on exporting and importing endangered animals under CITES have been successful in eliminating much of the trade in jaguar skins but not all of it.

Jaguars vs. Livestock

Although jaguars are still occasionally hunted for sport as much as for their beautiful skins, most of the big cats being killed in sizable numbers are being killed by ranchers. This still happens in places where jaguars live or range close to livestock. In many places, ranchers established cattle ranches in the jaguar's traditional habitat. By doing that, the prey that jaguars feed on were eliminated to a great extent, and without prey, jaguars turned to the only available food source—cattle—to survive. There is another reason jaguars kill cattle. In many parts of the jaguar's range, people hunt animals such as peccaries, tapirs, and deer. In

effect, they are competing with the jaguar for the big cat's preferred sources of food. Indeed, the hunting of jaguar prey is a real threat to the continued survival of jaguars. So the jaguar turns to cattle, when necessary. Because of this, ranchers do not hesitate to shoot jaguars on sight.

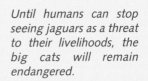

Until humans can stop seeing jaguars as a threat to their livelihoods, the big cats will remain endangered.

In Arizona and New Mexico during the first quarter of the twentieth century, many of the jaguars that were killed were shot by ranchers. Many of those ranchers were small homesteaders for whom the loss of a single cow or steer proved to be a great hardship. That situation has not changed in many parts of the jaguar's range today.

Poison

Sometimes, jaguars are poisoned by ranchers. The following incident was reported in 1931 by Vernon Bailey in Mammals of New Mexico:

> Mrs. Manning had been in the habit of putting out poison to kill the predatory animals about the ranch . . . and among the victims of the poisoned baits was this jaguar, which had been killing stock on the ranch for some time. It had killed 17 calves near the house during a short period before it was secured. The ranch was located at about 9,000 feet altitude in the pine and spruce timber of this exceedingly rough range of mountains.[2]

Regardless of the laws within each country, the killing of jaguars continues as long as ranchers and farmers think killing them is the only way to protect their livestock and livelihood. And in most countries, the laws against killing jaguars are not strictly enforced on the local level. In Sonora in northern Mexico, for example, cattle range practically everywhere. Some of them are partly wild and have become part of the area's ecosystem. Those cattle are now a regular part of the jaguar's diet. This is true even in areas where traditional jaguar prey, such as the white-tailed deer and the javelina, a piglike animal, are common. As long as cattle are being killed by jaguars, ranchers will trap, hunt, and poison the big cats unless the ranchers can learn to live with them and make a living themselves.

▶ Coexistence Is the Key

Recent research by members of the Wildlife Conservation Society's Jaguar Conservation Program has shown things can be done in the

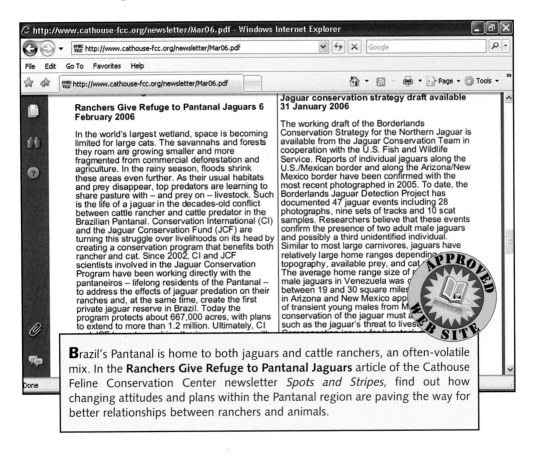

Ranchers Give Refuge to Pantanal Jaguars 6 February 2006

In the world's largest wetland, space is becoming limited for large cats. The savannahs and forests they roam are growing smaller and more fragmented from commercial deforestation and agriculture. In the rainy season, floods shrink these areas even further. As their usual habitats and prey disappear, top predators are learning to share pasture with – and prey on – livestock. Such is the life of a jaguar in the decades-old conflict between cattle rancher and cattle predator in the Brazilian Pantanal. Conservation International (CI) and the Jaguar Conservation Fund (JCF) are turning this struggle over livelihoods on its head by creating a conservation program that benefits both rancher and cat. Since 2002, CI and JCF scientists involved in the Jaguar Conservation Program have been working directly with the pantaneiros – lifelong residents of the Pantanal – to address the effects of jaguar predation on their ranches and, at the same time, create the first private jaguar reserve in Brazil. Today the program protects about 667,000 acres, with plans to extend to more than 1.2 million. Ultimately, CI

Jaguar conservation strategy draft available 31 January 2006

The working draft of the Borderlands Conservation Strategy for the Northern Jaguar is available from the Jaguar Conservation Team in cooperation with the U.S. Fish and Wildlife Service. Reports of individual jaguars along the U.S./Mexican border and along the Arizona/New Mexico border have been confirmed with the most recent photographed in 2005. To date, the Borderlands Jaguar Detection Project has documented 47 jaguar events including 28 photographs, nine sets of tracks and 10 scat samples. Researchers believe that these events confirm the presence of two adult male jaguars and possibly a third unidentified individual. Similar to most large carnivores, jaguars have relatively large home ranges depending topography, available prey, and cat. The average home range size of male jaguars in Venezuela was between 19 and 30 square miles in Arizona and New Mexico app of transient young males from M conservation of the jaguar must such as the jaguar's threat to lives

Brazil's Pantanal is home to both jaguars and cattle ranchers, an often-volatile mix. In the **Ranchers Give Refuge to Pantanal Jaguars** article of the Cathouse Feline Conservation Center newsletter *Spots and Stripes,* find out how changing attitudes and plans within the Pantanal region are paving the way for better relationships between ranchers and animals.

communities where jaguars live so that humans and jaguars can coexist. In areas where livestock management can be improved so that cattle production is increased, as in the Pantanal of Brazil, ranchers have shown that they can tolerate a certain amount of their cattle being killed by jaguars. Conservation groups are now working with ranchers and farmers in such areas to learn about the losses they suffer from jaguars, monitor the mount of livestock lost to the big cats, and most importantly, to put into practice measures to decrease conflicts between humans and jaguars.

▶ Lessening Livestock Losses

Ranchers have shown an interest in ecotourism, at least on a small scale, as long as that activity brings money into the community itself. They have also shown a willingness to experiment with nonlethal methods of keeping jaguars away from their cattle. Even in Belize, where nearly half of the country's territory provides protection for wildlife, jaguars are still being killed by livestock owners. Here as elsewhere, those owners often retaliate against jaguars whether they own a small farm made up of chickens and pigs or a large ranch consisting of thousands of head of cattle. Conservationists are working in the countries where jaguars live to help communities by suggesting techniques to lessen livestock losses.

In some areas, conservation groups have gotten together to come up with other solutions to the jaguar-human conflict. Some farmers in Brazil's Pantanal are now being paid (by a program run by Conservation International and the Earthwatch Institute) for each head of cattle killed by jaguars or pumas. In return for that payment, the farmers have pledged not to kill these predators for two years. Jaguars and pumas are feared in the region because they are such efficient hunters.

▷ Loss of Habitat

Even if ranchers or poachers did not kill jaguars, a major threat to the big cats' existence remains:

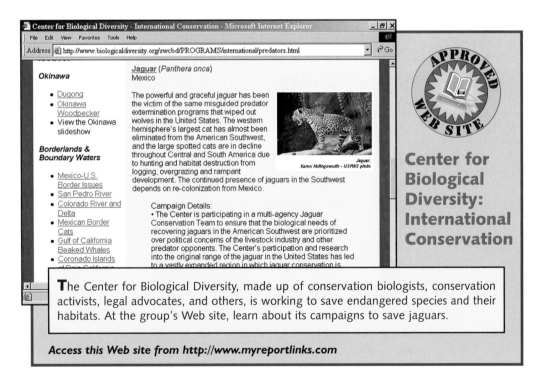

The Center for Biological Diversity, made up of conservation biologists, conservation activists, legal advocates, and others, is working to save endangered species and their habitats. At the group's Web site, learn about its campaigns to save jaguars.

Access this Web site from http://www.myreportlinks.com

Jaguars are losing their homes at an alarming rate. Loss of habitat is almost always the major reason that species become endangered, and that is certainly true in the jaguar's case.

Many of the rain forests, jungles, and grasslands of Central and South America have been developed or turned into farms in recent years. These once-wild places supported a tremendous diversity of animal and plant life. With development, however, trees have been cut down, native animals have been displaced, and the delicate balance that exists in a healthy rain-forest ecosystem has been upset. Each year, human settlement and human activities, such as mining, logging, cattle ranching, and road building, carve out more and more of the jaguar's habitat. In some parts of Brazil and Venezuela, the only jaguar habitat remaining outside of protected areas is on large expanses of cattle land or other private landholdings.

Development vs. Conservation

In Sonora, Mexico, the remote Huasabas-Sahuaripa area has been home to jaguars for a long time. But plans are being drawn up for large-scale development that will have a disastrous impact on the jaguars and other wildlife living there. More dams may be constructed on several of the area's rivers, including Ríos Bavispe, Yaqui, and Aros.[3] If those dams are built, more roads will

Wildlife Matters, a Web page of the Philadelphia Zoo, describes the Mexico Jaguar Project, a collaboration between the zoo and Mexican conservation organizations to save these big cats south of the border from extinction.

need to be built also. This will in turn make the region more accessible to people. With roads in place, mining companies will undoubtedly look to exploit the area's rich natural resources. A plan for a series of open-pit mines is already on the drawing boards. What is happening in Huasabas-Sahuaripa is not unique, unfortunately. The same kind of thing is happening in many other areas of jaguar habitat.

To many people, especially those who stand to make money from such development, this is considered progress. For others, especially conservationists, it is anything but. They understand that the loss of the jaguar to an ecosystem makes that ecosystem less healthy overall—and may bring about the extinction of many other species within it.

When even just parts of the jaguar's habitat are developed, the habitat as a whole becomes fragmented. That fragmentation means it is harder to sustain a healthy population of animals. As jaguars interact more with unvaccinated domestic cats and dogs and livestock, the risk of spreading disease to the jaguar population increases. The loss of habitat combined with greater vulnerability to disease continues to be a major threat to the jaguar's survival.

CURRENT EFFORTS TO PROTECT THE SPECIES

The effort to save the jaguar involves local and federal governments, conservation groups, scientists, and private citizens. Research on jaguars and jaguar habitats is ongoing. Current jaguar conservation efforts include habitat preservation and restoration, captive breeding, public education, and sometimes translocation (moving the cats from one location to another one considered safer).

Dr. Alan Rabinowitz is responsible for organizing and inspiring much of this work. In the early 1980s, Rabinowitz studied jaguars in the rain forests of Belize. There he helped to establish the world's first jaguar preserve in the Cockscomb Basin Wildlife Sanctuary. The government of Belize set aside 150 square miles (388 square kilometers) of rain forest for that purpose. The Cockscomb Basin preserve currently provides a protected environment for about two hundred jaguars, the largest concentration of jaguars in the world.

The difficulty with establishing preserves is that jaguars have a tendency to wander long distances throughout their range. The big cats are not always

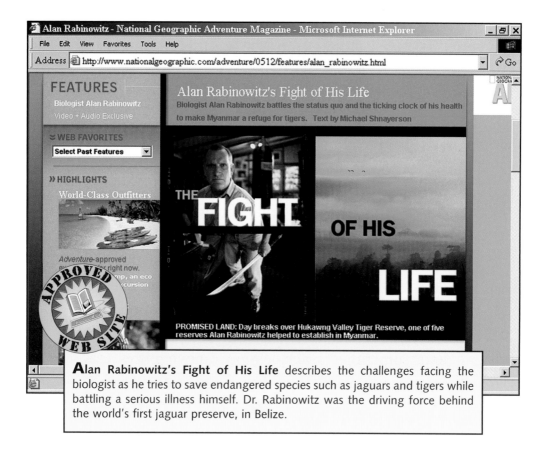

Alan Rabinowitz's Fight of His Life describes the challenges facing the biologist as he tries to save endangered species such as jaguars and tigers while battling a serious illness himself. Dr. Rabinowitz was the driving force behind the world's first jaguar preserve, in Belize.

inclined to stay within the boundaries of parks. Writing more than twenty years ago, Alan Rabinowitz expressed his concern that not enough was being done to save the jaguar:

> We sit by and allow massive destruction of the jaguar's habitat, forcing it into situations where death is the inevitable conclusion. Yet even as we are destroying it, we admire the animal—in zoos, on television, in books—and we wonder how it lives, what it eats, not even stopping to think it might soon no longer be living or eating at all. Then when the jaguar's gone from the wild, we'll carve its image in stone and speculate about how

magnificent it must have been. . . . In half a century, will the only live jaguars be in zoos? These animals who can walk miles at night through the jungle stalking a peccary herd want nothing more than to be left alone. When the jaguar no longer walks the forests, there will never be anything on earth like it again.[1]

The good news, though, is that progress has been made since 1986, when Rabinowitz wrote those words, although the fight to save jaguars from extinction is a long way from being won.

Programs for Saving the Jaguar

The Wildlife Conservation Society (WCS) has been working to save the great cats on an international scale for decades. Led by Dr. Rabinowitz, Executive Director of the WCS Science and Exploration Program, the Great Cat Program, established in 1989, builds on important studies by Dr. George Schaller and others on jaguars, lions, tigers, and snow leopards. The program's mission is to advance our knowledge of these species and develop strategies for their conservation as well as the preservation of the habitats they occupy.

In March 1999, thirty-five of the world's jaguar experts met in Mexico at the Jaguars in the New Millennium workshop. They gathered to assess the status and distribution of jaguars across their range and to determine the best way to conserve

Endangered Species in the Malpai Borderlands Region - Microsoft Internet Explorer

File   Edit   View   Favorites   Tools   Help

Address http://www.malpaiborderlandsgroup.org/endg.asp   Go

Our Roots

Land Protection

Land Management

Fire

Endangered Species

Science

Public Outreach

Resources

Site Photos by the Malpai B----- -----roup

experts. Our region has one of the highest number of listed species known from any comparable area, with near 30 endangered species that live here full time, or migrate through during part of the year. When we thought about endangered species at all, it was mostly to wonder what problems they would cause for us. We certainly didn't think of them as an asset. However, one-by-one, need arose to learn more about our listed species. The Malpai Group's efforts have gradually taken a leading role in developing information about the ecology and management needs for several species. We discovered that in some situations their presence can actually be an aid to achieving our landscape goals.

To read more about our efforts in working with endangered species, click here.

The federally-listed endangered species known to be found in the Malpai area are detailed in the following table. In addition, Peter Warren has written an informative article on the planning efforts of MBG to create a multi-specie Habitat Conservation Plan to protect the threatened and endangered species that are found at the Malpai. If you would like to read his article, click here.

| | **Chiricahua Leopard Frog** | One of the first endangered species projects the Group got involved with was to help the Magoffin family develop reliable water for a Chiricahua leopard frog population. Beginning in 1994 a stock ta...read more |
| | | In early spring of 1996, Warner Glenn and his daughter Kelly were on a mountain lion hunt in ...when ... |

APPROVED WEB SITE

The **Malpai Borderlands Group** is a grassroots organization of landowners in Arizona and New Mexico trying to save and restore nearly 1 million acres of open space lands. In doing so, the group has also become involved in saving the endangered species, such as jaguars, that are found in this vast area.

them. The workshop was supported by the National Autonomous University of Mexico and Jaguar USA cars. Upon discussing the status of jaguars across their range, the experts concluded that 21 percent of the jaguar range is threatened by a variety of factors. They also developed plans to conduct an assessment of long-term jaguar survival in all of the jaguar habitats. The results of this meeting provided the framework for the WCS Jaguar Conservation Program (JCP).

The JCP consists of the following components: jaguar population status and distribution surveys, establishment of long-term ecological studies of jaguars in various habitats and across a range of human impacts, jaguar-livestock conflicts and rancher outreach, jaguar population monitoring, jaguar health and genetics studies, and education and policy initiatives.

The program has ambitious goals. More than just saving a few wild jaguars in a few important but isolated areas, it is trying to save jaguars everywhere. As Alan Rabinowitz describes the mission, it is "to save jaguars throughout their entire range, from Mexico to Argentina, by creating and securing a natural corridor on public and private lands where jaguars can thrive well into the future."[2]

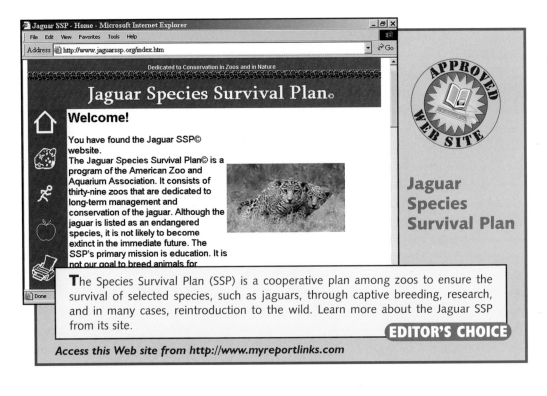

The Species Survival Plan (SSP) is a cooperative plan among zoos to ensure the survival of selected species, such as jaguars, through captive breeding, research, and in many cases, reintroduction to the wild. Learn more about the Jaguar SSP from its site.

EDITOR'S CHOICE

Access this Web site from http://www.myreportlinks.com

By saving their habitat and learning to live peacefully with them, we can save jaguars from disappearing from the earth forever.

Scientists in various places are trying to end the conflict between ranchers and jaguars. In Sonora, Mexico, cattle roam the range without restriction. It is not easy to persuade ranchers there to change their traditional way of ranching. But scientists hope to persuade ranchers to keep their cattle in fenced-in grazing land. This should result in less contact between jaguars and the ranchers and their cattle.

Recently, Mexico and Venezuela began exploring the possibility of offering "green" jaguar hunts. The Safari Club International (SCI) has a new category for hunters of the big cats who want to pursue these trophy animals—darted jaguar. Instead of shooting a jaguar with bullets from a rifle, the hunter pays a fee for the opportunity to chase and shoot the big cat with immobilizing drugs. The drugged jaguar is then radio collared and monitored as part of a research project. This program is controversial and is not supported by many conservationists, however.

There are reasons to believe that if at least some of the many efforts being carried out to protect the jaguar are successful, the big cat will survive. In the future, those brave souls venturing into jaguar habitat may yet be rewarded with a glimpse of *el tigre.*

In 1973, Congress took the farsighted step of creating the Endangered Species Act, widely regarded as the world's strongest and most effective wildlife conservation law. It set an ambitious goal: to reverse the alarming trend of human-caused extinction that threatened the ecosystems we all share.

Each book in this series explores the life of an endangered animal. The books tell how and why the animals have become endangered and explain the efforts being made to restore their populations.

The United States Fish and Wildlife Service and the National Marine Fisheries Service share responsibility for administration of the Endangered Species Act. Over time, animals are added to, reclassified in, or removed from the federal list of Endangered and Threatened Wildlife and Plants. At the time of publication, all the animals in this series were listed as endangered species. The most up-to-date list can be found at **http://www.fws.gov/endangered/wildlife.html**.

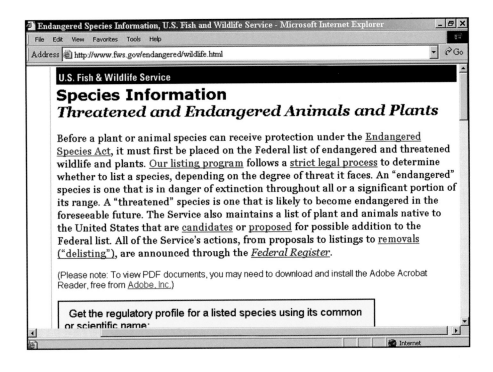

Report Links

The Internet sites described below can be accessed at
http://www.myreportlinks.com

▶**Save the Jaguar**
Editor's Choice The Wildlife Conservation Society is at the forefront of jaguar conservation.

▶**Phantoms of the Night**
Editor's Choice This *National Geographic* site explores the jaguar through various media.

▶**Jaguar Species Survival Plan**
Editor's Choice Zoos cooperate to protect jaguars through the SSP.

▶**ARKive: Jaguar (*Panthera onca*)**
Editor's Choice View photographs of the jaguar on this Web site.

▶**Journey Into Amazonia**
Editor's Choice Explore one of Earth's natural wonders—the Amazon region—at this site.

▶**Northern Jaguar Project**
Editor's Choice Read about one of the most ambitious projects yet to save jaguars.

▶**Alan Rabinowitz's Fight of His Life**
Find out more about the wildlife biologist who has helped to save jaguars and other big cats.

▶**Arizona Game & Fish: Jaguar Conservation**
Find out about the Arizona Game & Fish Department's efforts to save the jaguar.

▶**Big Cat Rescue: Jaguar**
Read about a rescue organization's work to save the jaguar.

▶**Big Cats**
This WWF article discusses the conservation of big cats around the world.

▶**Cat on the Spot**
A National Wildlife Federation online resource offering an overview of three endangered cats.

▶**Center for Biological Diversity: International Conservation**
The Center for Biological Diversity's campaigns are attempting to save wild places and wildlife.

▶**Connecting the Dots**
Wildlife Conservation magazine features a story on jaguar endangerment.

▶**"Ghost Cat"**
This *Audubon* magazine article looks at the jaguar in the United States.

▶**"Is the Big Cat Back?"**
Defenders magazine offers this article on new conservation measures for the jaguar.

Report Links

The Internet sites described below can be accessed at
http://www.myreportlinks.com

▶**IUCN Red List of Threatened Species**
This is a list of the world's threatened and endangered species.

▶**Jaguar**
This Defenders of Wildlife site looks at the plight of the jaguar.

▶**Jaguar: Lord of the Mayan Jungle**
Take an online tour of the land of the Maya and meet the resident jaguars.

▶**Jaguar (Panthera onca)**
Visit a zoo and wildlife museum that is home to a variety of wild cat species.

▶**Malpai Borderlands Group**
Visit the site of a group of Southwesterners trying to protect land and the species it contains.

▶**People of the Jaguar**
A Canadian museum site explores the connection between jaguars and the ancient Maya.

▶**Ranchers Give Refuge to Pantanal Jaguars**
Conservation International explores the connection between ranchers and jaguars.

▶**Reproductive Technologies and Conservation of Endangered Cats**
Learn how the National Zoo is meeting the challenge of saving endangered big cats.

▶**"Return of the Jaguar?"**
A reappearance of the elusive jaguar in Arizona is the focus of this *Smithsonian* magazine article.

▶**San Diego Zoo's Animal Bytes: Jaguar**
Find a zoo's overview of the jaguar on this site.

▶**Sierra Club—Endangered Species Act**
This conservation organization works to protect natural ecosystems around the world.

▶**USFWS Endangered Species Program Kid's Corner**
This USFWS Web page offers ways you can help save endangered species.

▶**A Vibrant Landscape**
This PBS online treatment examines the history of the jaguar.

▶**WAN Conservancy: Can We Bring Back the Jaguar?**
A conservation group works to bring jaguars back to the United States.

▶**Wildlife Matters**
Read about the Philadelphia Zoo's efforts to save jaguars.

ambush—As a noun, a place where an animal or person hides before a surprise attack.

Beringia—The land bridge across the Bering Strait that connected Siberia and Alaska during ice ages when the sea level dropped.

caiman—A South American cousin of the crocodile.

camouflage—Coloring and special markings that enable an animal to blend in perfectly with its forest surroundings and allow it to become almost invisible to its prey.

capybara—The world's largest rodent.

carnivore—An animal that eats meat.

causeway—A raised road or pathway that allows people to travel over water or wet, soggy land. Cockscomb Basin Wildlife

Cockscomb Basin Wildlife Sanctuary—The world's only jaguar preserve, established in Belize in 1984 with the help of Dr. Alan Rabinowitz.

conservation—Preservation or management of a natural resource or plant and animal species.

ecology—The study of the environment and how plant and animal species relate to it.

habitat—The place where an animal or a plant normally lives.

home range—The area of land used by an animal throughout its life.

Jaguar Knights—An elite military order of Aztec warriors.

Kinich Ahau—The Maya sun god who transformed himself into a jaguar during his nightly journey through the underworld.

La Brea Tar Pits—The richest deposit of ice-age fossils in the world, located in Los Angeles, California.

melanistic jaguar—A black jaguar.

montane habitat—Relatively cool, moist upland slopes covered by evergreen forests.

nocturnal—Active at night.

peccary—A piglike animal with razor-sharp tusks.

rosettes—Black, ringlike markings on the skin of the jaguar.

savanna—A large area of grassy plains.

shaman—A medicine man in a tribal culture.

species—A group of organisms so similar to one another that they can interbreed.

tapetum—The layer of reflecting cells at the back of the jaguar's eye.

tapir—A nocturnal hoofed mammal related to horses and rhinos with short limbs and a fleshy snout.

Tezcatlipoca—An Aztec god usually depicted as a jaguar.

translocation—The moving of animals to new areas.

were-jaguar—A creature that is half jaguar, half human.

Chapter 1. Encounters With Jaguars

1. Aldo Starker Leopold (1959) *Wildlife of Mexico,* as quoted in David E. Brown and Carlos A. López González, *Borderland Jaguars (Tigres de la Frontera)* (Salt Lake City: The University of Utah Press, 2001), p. 1.

2. Fiona Sunquist, "Jaguar," in *Kingdom of Cats* (Washington, D.C.: National Wildlife Federation, 1987), p. 61.

3. Alan Rabinowitz, *Jaguar: One Man's Battle to Establish the World's First Jaguar Preserve* (New York: Anchor Books, 1986), p. 284.

4. Ibid., p. 285.

5. U.S. Fish and Wildlife Service, *Endangered Species Bulletin,* March 2006.

Chapter 2. Jaguar Habitat and Range, Past and Present

1. David E. Brown and Carlos A. López González, *Borderland Jaguars (Tigres de la Frontera)* (Salt Lake City: The University of Utah Press, 2001), p. 31.

2. A. Starker Leopold (1959) *Wildlife of Mexico,* as quoted in David E. Brown and Carlos A. López González, *Borderland Jaguars (Tigres de la Frontera)* (Salt Lake City: The University of Utah Press, 2001), p. 43.

3. Fiona Sunquist, "Jaguar," in *Kingdom of Cats* (Washington, D.C.: National Wildlife Federation, 1987), p. 65.

4. Brown and González, p. 4.

Chapter 3. Physical Characteristics of Jaguars

1. C.A.W. Guggisberg, *Wild Cats of the World* (New York: Taplinger Publishing Company, 1975), p. 248.

2. Les Line and Edward R. Ricciuti, *The Audubon Society Book of Wild Cats* (New York: Harry N. Abrams, Inc., 1985), p. 180.

3. Guggisberg, p. 263.

Chapter 4. Jaguar Behavior

1. C.A.W. Guggisberg, *Wild Cats of the World* (New York: Taplinger Publishing Company, 1975), p. 262.

2. Ibid., p. 263.

3. E. W. Nelson, as quoted in David E. Brown and Carlos A. López González, *Borderland Jaguars (Tigres de la Frontera)* (Salt Lake City: The University of Utah Press, 2001), p. 32.

4. A. Starker Leopold (1959) *Wildlife of Mexico,* as quoted in David E. Brown and Carlos A. López González, *Borderland Jaguars (Tigres de la Frontera)* (Salt Lake City: The University of Utah Press, 2001), pp. 42–43.

5. Fiona Sunquist, "Jaguar," in *Kingdom of Cats* (Washington, D.C.: National Wildlife Federation, 1987), p. 64.

6. Guggisberg, p. 255.

7. Ibid., p. 256.

8. Ibid., p. 257.

9. Ibid., p. 260.

Chapter 5. The Jaguar in Human Cultures

1. Alan Rabinowitz, *Jaguar: One Man's Battle to Establish the World's First Jaguar Preserve* (New York: Anchor Books, 1986), p. 286.

2. Fiona Sunquist, "Jaguar," in *Kingdom of Cats* (Washington, D.C.: National Wildlife Federation, 1987), p. 61.

3. Tony Burton, "One Day in Oaxaca = Two Thousand Years . . . Part 2: A Self-Guided Tour of Monte Alban and the Zimatlan Valley," *Tony Burton's Do It Yourself Tours,* 1998, <http://www.mexconnect.com/mex_/travel/tonysarticles/tboaxaca2.html> (July 6, 2007).

4. David E. Brown and Carlos A. Lopez Gonzalez, *Borderland Jaguars (Tigres de la Frontera)* (Salt Lake City: The University of Utah Press, 2001), p. 76.

Chapter 6. Threats to the Cats' Survival

1. "The Fauna of Arizona," *Mining and Scientific Press* (March 3, 1883), as quoted in David E. Brown and Carlos A. López González, *Borderland Jaguars (Tigres de la Frontera)* (Salt Lake City: The University of Utah Press, 2001), p. 15.

2. Vernon Bailey (1931) *Mammals of New Mexico,* as quoted in David E. Brown and Carlos A. López González, *Borderland Jaguars (Tigres de la Frontera)* (Salt Lake City: The University of Utah Press, 2001), p. 89.

3. David E. Brown and Carlos A. López González, *Borderland Jaguars (Tigres de la Frontera)* (Salt Lake City: The University of Utah Press, 2001), p. 110.

Chapter 7. Current Efforts to Protect the Species

1. Alan Rabinowitz, *Jaguar: One Man's Battle to Establish the World's First Jaguar Preserve* (New York: Anchor Books 1986), p. 292.

2. Alan Rabinowitz, *Wildlife Conservation Society, Save the Jaguars,* "An Important Appeal From Dr. Alan Rabinowitz," n.d., <http://savethejaguar.com/jag-index/jagappeal> (March 15, 2007).

Baquedano, Elizabeth. *Aztec, Inca, and Maya.* New York: DK Publishing, 2005.

Bauer, Erwin. *The Last Big Cats: An Untamed Spirit.* Stillwater, Minn.: Voyageur Press, 2003.

Hare, Tony. *Animal Habitats: Discovering How Animals Live in the Wild.* New York: Facts On File, 2001.

Lalley, Pat. *Jaguars.* Austin, Tex.: Steck-Vaughn, 2000.

Malaspina, Ann. *The Jaguar.* Farmington Hills, Mich.: Lucent Books, 2000.

Miles, Victoria. *Wild Science: Amazing Encounters Between Animals and the People Who Study Them.* Berkeley, Calif.: Raincoast Books, 2004.

Patent, Dorothy Hinshaw. *Big Cats.* New York: Walker & Co., 2005

Penny, Malcom. *Endangered Species: Our Impact on the Planet.* Austin, Tex.: Raintree Steck-Vaughn Publishers, 2002.

Squire, Ann O. *Jaguars.* New York: Scholastic, 2005.

Stille, Darlene R. *Jaguars.* Minneapolis: Compass Point Books, 2001.

Tagliaferro, Lisa. *Explore the Tropical Rain Forest.* Mankato, Minn.: Capstone Press, 2007.

Thomas, Peggy. *Big Cat Conservation.* Brookfield, Conn.: Twenty-First Century Books, 2000.